The Arbuthnot Lectures

1980–1989

May Hill Arbuthnot
1884–1969

The Arbuthnot Lectures

1980–1989

ASSOCIATION FOR LIBRARY
SERVICE TO CHILDREN

American Library Association
CHICAGO AND LONDON 1990

The paper used in this publication meets the minimum requirements of American National Standard for Information Sciences—Permanence of Paper for Printed Library Materials, ANSI Z39.48-1984. ∞

Library of Congress Cataloging-in-Publication Data

The Arbuthnot lectures, 1980–1989 / Association for Library Service to Children.
p. cm.
ISBN 0-8389-3388-2
1. Children's literature—History and criticism. I. Association for Library Service to Children.
PN1009.A1A74 1990
809'.89282—dc20 90-37162

Printed in the United States of America.

94 93 92 91 90 5 4 3 2 1

Contents

The May Hill Arbuthnot Honor Lectureship

This annual lectureship honors May Hill Arbuthnot, an authority on literature for children. Funded by Scott, Foresman and Company and administered by the Association for Library Service to Children (ALSC) of the American Library Association, this free public lecture is presented annually by a distinguished author, critic, librarian, historian, or teacher of children's literature. The lectures are given between late March and early May. The text of each lecture is subsequently published in ALSC's *Journal of Youth Services in Libraries* (formerly *Top of the News*).

The Background

Scott, Foresman and Company, the chief publisher of May Hill Arbuthnot's many books, proposed in 1968 to the Children's Services Division (now the Association for Library Service to Children) of the American Library Association that it become the administrator of an award to be funded by the company in honor of May Hill Arbuthnot's outstanding contributions to children's literature. After extensive and careful deliberation, the division proposed that a lecture series be established. Officials at Scott, Foresman concurred with enthusiasm. In 1969, plans were made for the first lecture to be given at Western Reserve (subsequently Case Western Reserve) University in Cleveland, Ohio, where May Hill Arbuthnot taught between 1927 and 1949.

Each year the vice-president/president-elect of the Association for Library Service to Children appoints a five-person committee from ALSC membership to select and invite each lecturer. The announcement of the lecturer for the following year is made annually at the Midwinter Meeting of the American Library Association. A library, library school or department of education in a college or university, a public library system, or a cooperative coalition of such agencies may apply to host the lecture. Competition is always keen. Plans to host the lecture are proposed annually by libraries and library-related institutions in all regions of the United States. The host site selected by the committee from the applications is announced during the ALA's Annual Conference.

This Collection of Lectures

This collection of Arbuthnot lectures is the second published by the American Library Association. The first appeared in 1980 and contained the lectures given between 1969 and 1979. The collection here spans the second decade of the lectureship. This volume contains the Arbuthnot lectures of Horst J. Kunze (East Germany), Virginia Betancourt (Venezuela), Dorothy Butler (New Zealand), Leland B. Jacobs (U.S.A.), Fritz Eichenberg (U.S.A.), Patricia Wrightson (Australia), Aidan Chambers (England), James Houston (Canada), John Bierhorst (U.S.A.), and Margaret Mahy (New Zealand). Host sites during this decade were in Wisconsin, Texas, Florida, Georgia, Minnesota, Indiana, Arkansas, Illinois, Oklahoma, and Pennsylvania.

Throughout the 1980s, the field of children's literature expanded and changed, as did library services for children. Significant opportunity for the continuing professional development of librarians and others working professionally with children and with children's literature was consistently available through the provision of the annual Arbuthnot lectureship.

During the ALA meeting in 1969 at which the first lectureship was announced, May Hill Arbuthnot spoke of her delight with the manner in which she was to be honored: "[I am] a strong believer in the efficacy of direct speech, the spoken word, . . . [This lectureship] means we shall be hearing new voices speak with new insight and new emphasis in this field of children's literature." This second collection of the lectures given in May Hill Arbuthnot's honor expands the audience for each lecture, offering such voices and emphases to readers interested in the many insights in children's literature provided by the Arbuthnot lecturers of the 1980s.

GINNY MOORE KRUSE

May Hill Arbuthnot

May Hill Arbuthnot, born in Mason City, Iowa, in 1884, spent part of her childhood in Massachusetts and Illinois. She specialized in kindergarten and primary education, receiving her degree at the University of Chicago in 1922. There she met the eminent educator William Scott Gray, who was later to become her colleague in writing textbooks for children at Scott, Foresman. The books, the Curriculum Foundation Readers, became better known as the "Dick and Jane" series, and were more widely used than widely acclaimed. Perhaps because of this, *Children and Books,* Mrs. Arbuthnot's own textbook, was not universally welcomed when its first edition appeared in 1947. Some critics felt that the author, as an educator, placed too much emphasis on function and not enough on literary merit.

As time passed and subsequent editions appeared, however, Mrs. Arbuthnot's high standards of evaluation, her insistence on the prime importance of literary quality, and her concern for giving children the best in world literature won recognition, and the book, in its revised editions, is still the best-selling textbook on children's literature published in the United States. Her work was characterized by a sense of dedication, a joy in sharing the best in children's books, and a zeal tempered by her understanding of the practical problems in bringing children and books together.

Mrs. Arbuthnot received her master's degree from Columbia University in 1924. In 1927, joining the faculty at Western Reserve University in Cleveland, she helped establish the first nursery schools there. The kindergarten-primary training school of which she was the principal became the university's department of elementary education. At Western Reserve, now Case Western Reserve University, she met and married Charles Arbuthnot, a professor in the economics department. Mrs. Arbuthnot retired in 1949 and spent many quiet, busy years writing, reviewing, lecturing, and participating in several professional organizations. She died in a Cleveland nursing home on October 2, 1969.

Mrs. Arbuthnot served as the review editor of children's books for the magazines *Childhood Education* and *Elementary English* (now *Language Arts*). Among her major works, most of which appeared in several editions, were *The Arbuthnot Anthology of Children's Literature* and *Children's Reading in the Home,* published by Scott, Foresman (as was, and is, *Children and Books*) and *Children's Books Too Good to Miss,* published by Western Reserve University Press, and subsequently by the University Press Book Service, Indiana University.

Among the honors she received were election to Phi Beta Kappa, Pi Lambda Theta, and Delta Kappa Gamma. In 1959, she received the Constance Lindsay Skinner Medal, given by the Women's National Book Association for a distinguished contribution to the field of books. Western Reserve University awarded her the Doctor of Humane Letters degree in 1961. In 1964 the Catholic Library Association awarded her the Regina Medal for distinguished contributions to the field of children's literature.

A woman of warmth and compassion, of flexibility and humor, May Hill Arbuthnot was distinguished for that rare quality, a truly open mind. A wise and blithe spirit, she has made a permanent and significant contribution to children's literature.

ZENA SUTHERLAND

Horst J. Kunze

German Children's Literature from Its Beginning to the Nineteenth Century

A HISTORICAL PERSPECTIVE

Horst J. Kunze

a scholar and bibliographer of children's literature, is director emeritus of the Deutsche Staatsbibliotek in Berlin, German Democratic Republic. Kunze is recognized for his professional contributions concerning rare books. His publications include the definitive *Schatzbehalter alter Kinderbucher*, a critical and historical appraisal of nineteenth-century German illustrators; a work on Werner Klemke, a contemporary East German children's book illustrator; and the *Geschichte Der Buchillustration in Deutschland*.

THE HISTORY OF EUROPEAN LIBRARIES shows a dual, conflicting development in regard to children's books: since their beginnings in the nineteenth century public libraries have nurtured the children's and young people's book; yet for centuries research libraries have ignored this literature or have treated it as being of secondary importance. This development is not as curious as it seems at first sight if we consider the low respect literature commanded during the seventeenth and eighteenth centuries. Compared to the reception of literature in general, children's literature has come a long way.

Today there is no longer any serious doubt about the fact that the literature for children and young people is a part of the national literature. But there is often a discrepancy between theory and practice. In both German states, for instance, the Germanic philologists do not yet pay due attention to the book for children. Research work in this field is, as in former times, still largely left to pedagogues and librarians as well as to outsiders and amateurs.

Before dealing with my main theme, which is to try to show you the development of German literature for children from the beginning up to the nineteenth century, some principles have to be clarified.

1. *Terminology.* In German, two terms—"literature for children" and "literature for young people"—are often used incorrectly. Of these, only the term "literature for children" can be clearly conceived as being a specific part of national literature.

Based on the terminology of those concerned with the service area of children's library work we can determine that the book for children, written or illustrated by an author or artist for young readers, is intended for children up to the age of fourteen. As reading ability is a decisive factor for the understanding of literature and promotion of the child's self-awareness, we refer, within this group of books for children, to the literary products intended for the preschool age (that is, up to the age of six) as the first stage. The basic type of the first stage is the picture book without a text or with very little text.

Books for young people are generally considered for the age from fourteen to eighteen years. The relationship between text and illustration no longer follows a pattern as in books intended for the younger age group.

These differentiations also apply if we consider that, as in the whole life of man and in the development of the child, individual and environmental factors play an important role. First of all, within the pro-

---

Presented May 3, 1980, in Milwaukee, Wisconsin, by the Association for Library Service to Children in cooperation with the School of Library Science, University of Wisconsin–Milwaukee, and other agencies and institutions in Milwaukee.

cess of the reception of literature, there is the role of the adult reading to the child. The adult not only imparts additional texts to the picture book for the preschool age, but also introduces the next level of the children's reading—the children's book for the age from seven to fourteen. Of course, individual behavioral patterns, a child's receptivity, and his own developmental stage, which depend upon additional influences, e.g., the home, point out the flexibility of the abovementioned age designations of the books for children and young people.

These factors, e.g., the psychological, social development, etc., of the child, determine at what point each child passes from one category to the next, at what point a child might even be prematurely initiated to the book for young people, the popular book, and the book for adults.

If the transition from the children's book (age six to fourteen) to the book for young people is easily and often hurriedly made by children, the third step, from young people's book to the adult book, becomes even more apparent. The young adult is not only physically but socially in an in-between stage, between childhood and maturity. At this stage everything is in transition and on threshold. The adult author is speaking "from above" to young readers, whereas the author of books for adults directs his works to equals, writing for his own cause. The former must adopt a heterogeneous point of view and turn his thoughts back to the scope of experience which young people have.

These very difficult, inherent aspects of the book for young people indicate why there have been, and still are, so very few good books for young people. Literature for young people should be a guiding tool toward literature, the arts, and sciences, as well as to problems of life and of our times. One might even be inclined to maintain that due to the nature of its intended audience all literature for young people adheres to characteristics of its own. It is susceptible to a variety of factors. This may include books which are especially geared for the adolescent as well as appropriate adult books suitable for the recipient's developmental stage. In any case, it is far more difficult to determine the category of literature for young people than to determine the literature for preschool children, and this is also the reason for the existing terminological confusion in the field of literature for children and young people. And thus we have arrived at the inevitable interrelationship between literature and reading. The distribution and purchasing of books naturally follow the interests and needs of the reader.

2. *Basic Principles.* We must realize and understand the process of integrating children's with adult literature into a national literature. This integration will not be conceived correctly unless its inherent laws are understood in relation to the whole national literature on the one hand and the ideal of education, dependent on the period and the class concerned, on the other hand. Up to this day it is still not known well enough that the national literature is stratified according to literature for adults and literature for children. And we have become used

to identifying adult literature as "great" literature. Folk literature, at best, is at times classified with "great" literature; yet its research is separated from the mainstream of literature and left to folklorists. Since the eighteenth century another area of literature has been, and is still being, neglected. I am referring to the "consumer literature" (I refuse the term "trivial" literature which is commonly used in German-speaking countries) of contemporary and popular authors which exercises a very obvious influence over its own time. Since the late eighteenth century modern literature has produced not only hardcover books but also almanacs, pocket books, calendars, and journals. This same phenomenon also became apparent in the eighteenth and nineteenth centuries in the field of children's literature.

The whole complex of the national literature can be compared to a pyramid, the apex consisting of the "great" literature, labeled as "classical," the central part being dominated by folk literature and the best products of children's literature, and the broad lower zone comprising the popular, unpretentious fiction for adults and children.

Thus children's literature is always to be seen as closely related to the level reached by the national adult literature because literature for children and young people is part of a whole, of the national literature.

3. *Definition of Terms: "children's book" and "textbook."* Literature for children and young people is not identical with the textbook. Authors of textbooks view all age groups of the intended readership with the same perspective. The textbook is mainly characterized by its didactic purpose.

Literature for children and young people is developed when literature is written without this planned, didactic purpose. Yet, as the child's school and after-school activities cannot be sharply separated, children's books and textbooks overlap now and then, as well. This is obviously the case when excerpts from children's literature are included in educational texts (e.g., readers, history books) or in additional compulsory reading.

4. *International Links.* There are obvious links between literatures of different nations. Translations from foreign languages into a national language point this out. However, retrospective registration of translations does not suffice. Other links develop from influences, reception, or deliberate refusal of content and form of foreign literatures.

In addition to this, works of adult literature are adopted by children and young people—not only works of the national literature, but also translations from foreign literatures into the national literature. They are published either in the original form or in the form of editions revised for children and young people. It is perfectly justifiable to speak of conquest or adoption of adult books by children and young people. This process is still taking place in our time because it is based on the psychological motivation of children and young people: the attraction of the adult world and the resulting desire to conquer prematurely the books adults read, even though ample literature for children and young people is available. In modern times newspapers, trade journals, and general periodicals for adults—whether deliberately or not—encourage this desire of many children.

5. *Social Forces.* The creation of children's literature is caused by driving social forces within society. Any society creating and distributing literature for children and young people as a specific part of its national literature must have reached a certain level of development. A definite number of purchasers must be guaranteed; that is, a certain part of the ruling class must recognize the value, or at least the usefulness, of this branch of literature. As only adults create and buy literature for children and young people, concerned members of these ruling forces must be willing to invest a part of their product of labor in purchasing this literature for their children.

This, in turn, requires the development of a specific ideal of education which recognizes the child as an independent reader of literature and promotes literary activities in after-school environments. At this level of development society realizes that, apart from the child's duty to accept instruction or structured learning, the child also has the right to be entertained. Leisure reading, however, is by no means, and at least not from the beginning, distinct, but rather highly diffuse. Didactic, educational purposes can be quite easily combined with entertainment. In any case, the aim of adult education and the educational objectives concerning children depend primarily on the ruling classes of a society.

The development of children's literature is based on certain social factors, irrespective of national characteristics. Once these factors surface, they produce and then control the development of children's literature. A striking example of this process is found in Great Britain. There, various factors became effective initially, fostered by special conditions: the "Glorious Revolution" had brought victory over feudalism as early as 1688. The beginning of a specific literature for children in Great Britain can be dated almost to that very year. Before that, fables, textbooks, moral codes, and folk literature were, so to speak, available for everybody, including the small number of children of educated people who were able to read. In the eighteenth century, however, adult literature was tested by children and young people as being suitable for their own reading. Adaptations for children appeared. Richardson's novels, such as *Pamela,* are an example of this. Prior to this only instructive or deliberately didactic literature had been written expressly for children, but now, parallel to the *Pamela* adaptation, real children's literature was created, that is, a literature which for the first time was intended to amuse children.

John Newbery was the man who understood his time and the opportunities it offered for making money honestly. In 1745, he opened in London, the capital of his country, the first "Children's Bookshop" and became a publisher, a retail bookseller, and an author. His motto Instruction and Amusement of Children was, of course, not directed to the children themselves, but to their parents, who began to feel that they had to do something for the children of their rising class.

Having clarified these inherent aspects of children's literature, I shall now try to give you an outline of the development of the German book for children, although this outline must necessarily be extremely condensed.

Studies on the literature for children and young people based upon memoirs and autobiographical documents of great German personalities of the eighteenth and nineteenth centuries show some trends allowing for generalization. Of course, one must consider the personal and social factors evidenced in these documents.

For the last decades of the eighteenth century the following aspects became evident. The so-called "old comforters" were still customary in that period, that is, works of religious tradition, partly distributed in large and cheap editions as, for instance, prayer books, devotional books, and others of this kind. At the same time folk literature was very much alive, especially the German *Volksbücher* (popular chapbooks). In Goethe's *Poetry and Truth* (*Dichtung und Wahrheit*) we can see evidence of this. Finally, we take note of a comparatively large number of adult books more of a scientific than a *belletristic* nature. This manifests itself at first mainly in historical books, and later in more and more books about the natural sciences.

During the nineteenth century we observe an increase in specific literature for children and young people. Campe's *Robinson* and his *Children's Library* gained great influence that lasted far into the nineteenth century. Another important title, Schnabel's *Insel Felsenburg* (*Isle of the Rock Castle*), also emerged at that time. From the mid-nineteenth century on, German translations of Cooper's works demonstrate the great popularity of books about American Indians.

Another phenomenon is the development of distinguishably separate nonfiction for adults and for children.

These developments find their parallels in the history of German national literature and education. From the fifteenth century onward books were published that were accepted for children as well as for adults. Upon closer examination, they turn out to be aids for the teacher or educator. Some were intended for reading aloud, e.g., *Der Seele Trost* (*The Soul's Comfort,* Augsburg, 1478). After further examination this literature for children and young people frequently turns out to be folk literature. The close relationship between children's and young people's literature and folk literature from the beginning to the nineteenth century becomes evident. Folk literature was usually not received as a primary source but rather in the form of tales related by storytellers or as literary pieces meant for reading aloud. This trend continued into the nineteenth century.

Only in the second half of the eighteenth century do we find a wider and increasing readership of adult literature. The scope of the reading public cannot be compared to that of today, as it was still restricted mainly to the upper and middle classes. The novel or longer tale, often still referred to as a "story," began to grow into a new literary genre and find its readers among these strata in urban locations. At the same time a secularization of reading matter took place. Sermons and religious tracts, decreasing in the first half of the eighteenth century, found a new competitor in the novels, such as the English *Moral Weeklies,* which were being published widely. This explains why the new kind of literature, struggling for social recognition, was still striving for pious and moral justification. There are different opinions concerning the moral and didactic function of the novel. Yet there is wide agreement that the novel's purpose, at least up to the end of the eighteenth century, was to offer the reader moral guidance in an entertaining or even amusing manner.

We have to distinguish between literature for children and young people and the books which were actually read by children and young people. As a part of national literature, the literature for children and young people, intended in a restricted sense for children, mainly belonged to *belles lettres.* That means that it was subject to the rules of this literature. Since the late eighteenth century, the didactic book for children and young people, the textbook as well as the book for after-school reading, has played an increasingly important role. Today the nonfictional book for children and young people is considered to be an integral part of the general literature for children and young people.

In the nineteenth and twentieth centuries, the journal for young people most clearly represents the type of reading where entertaining *belles lettres* and didactic literature go hand in hand. A simple reason for this profuse and specific literary production has been the necessity to regularly fill the columns of these periodicals year after year.

Thus, in a broad sense, the literature for children and young people exceeds the fields of art, music, and aesthetics. It contributes to the dissemination of scientific knowledge founded on the motivation to establish a philosophy of life. Literature for children and young people comes into its own being when literary works for young readers are created, and when the author, in formulating his ideas and content, takes into account the developmental stage of his readers. In this sense, a specific literature for children and young people only came into being in Germany after the second half of the eighteenth century. And, from the eighteenth century to the present time, German children's literature can be divided into three groups.

Picture Books

The *Orbis Pictus* (1658) by Jan Amos Comenius is considered the first picture book and illustrated primer. It is, so to speak, the secularized branch of the part of folk literature characterized by the blockbook, e.g., the *Bible of the Poor.* The beginning of this development lies in the didactic textbook intended to prepare children for the demands of life. Pictures illustrate the information which was considered to be important for the child's position in his social class. We can observe a thread of progressive development beginning with this early picture book, leading to the different kinds of *orbis pictus* works created in the nineteenth century and finally to the contemporary children's encyclopedia. The picture story originating in the mid-nineteenth century was closely related to these synopses of knowledge enhanced by text and illustration. The prototype is *Shock-Headed Peter* (*Struwwelpeter*) by Heinrich Hoffman. Among the classics of this time are Wilhelm Busch's picture stories. But many other picture books such as those by Ludwig Richter, Oscar Pletsch, and Fedor Glinzer belong to this group as well.

The so-called art education movement of the nineteenth century consciously continued these great achievements in illustration. Then, at the turn of the century, the works of the Swiss artist and author Ernst Kreidolf were a climax. Other noteworthy picture book creators of this period were Freyhold, Osswald, and Wenz-Viëtor. Some publishers devoted themselves mainly to the picture book. One publishing house, Scholz of Mainz, even specialized in illustration of fairy tales. Apart from *Shock-Headed Peter,* the didactic features in picture books diminished in the second half of the nineteenth century. The artistic expression became the primary element. The picture book became an aesthetic means of instruction. A book for the real child was thus created, a book written without moral urgency but with the objective to entertain and involve the child.

Nursery Rhymes

The close relation to folk literature becomes very distinct in the nursery rhyme. The first collection of German nursery rhymes is an appendix to *Des Knaben Wunderhorn* (*The Boy's Magic Horn;* 1806–8), by Achim von Arnim and Clemens von Brentano. The Germanic philologist Karl Simrock added greatly to this type of literature with his collection *The German Nursery Rhyme* (1848). In the nineteenth century, the authors of nursery rhymes exploited this source, especially Hoffman von Fallersleben, but also Güll, Kopisch, and Reinick, and later Heinrich Seidel, Klaus Groth, and Gustav Falke.

Some of these collections of nursery rhymes skillfully combine text and illustrations, e.g., Friedrich Güll's *Kinderheimath in Liedern* (*Children's Home in Songs*) with Franz von Pocci's illustrations.

The advocate for the good children's book, Heinrich Wolgast himself, pays due attention to the nursery rhyme in his *Schöne alte Kinderreime* (*Fine Old Nursery Rhymes*). Even in our time these collections of old literary values play an important role in children's books.

Stories

The third group that can be described is the story. The underestimation of children's literature might be one of the reasons why in the nineteenth century only comparatively few great writers of literary works for adults also wrote for children. This field was therefore all the more cultivated by authors who either were urged by clever publishers (for instance, the writer Franz Hoffmann) or wrote because of a self-imposed calling (e.g., Christoph von Schmid, Gustav Nieritz, Karl May). Notable is the lack of literary achievement and quality especially when compared to the great quantity of inferior publications. Only those children's stories related to the reform movement show an improvement in literary quality. Some works of this type have remained of lasting value or are noteworthy only because of their illustrations (e.g., Theodor Hosemann).

As a final example, let us consider a special type of story, the fairy tale and the legend. This type again clearly shows the relationship with folk literature noted earlier. The *Kinder-und Hausmärchen* (*Fairy Tales for the Child and the Home*) by the Brothers Grimm with its child-oriented title may be considered a typical collection. Children's literature produced in the early period of the rise of the middle classes was governed by the trends of the period of "Enlightenment." Self-reliance, diligence, assiduity, obedience, and other civic, middle-class virtues including national pride became the goal of education for the children of the new bourgeois class. Following the victory of the new bourgeois class over feudalism, reactionary forces and nationalist as well as orthodox-religious trends adulterated this ideal of education. After the foundation of the "Reich" under Prussian hegemony, these factors became increasingly effective, even developing into chauvinism and racial arrogance. In addition, due to the growing technical improvements in book production, children's books became a profitable business. While many qualified people took part in it, others exploited the children's book market. These increasingly negative tendencies in children's book production became obvious in the neglect of content as well as format. The lack of quality brought about opposition from two fronts. The ruling powers themselves criticized literature for young people—a movement was led by Heinrich Wolgast, endorsed by committees for the improvement of young people's books. On the other hand, these reform tendencies met with the opposition of politically reactionary and clerically orthodox groups. In any case, it is to the credit of Wolgast and his apostles that literary criticism of children's books (almost nonexistent up to that time) was made a public concern.

Wolgast and the "angry young men" around him were politically associated with the working class. The working class itself, especially its more advanced strata, rejected the contents of the new literature for children. This class was beginning to be able to profit from the existing children's literature but was not yet strong enough in its own ranks to produce a working-class children's literature of its own.

Traditional bourgeois literature for children dominated the scene until 1918. From this date on, working class as well as bourgeois books for children were published in Germany.

We have thus traced the history of German children's books back again to our initial statement: the placement of children's literature within the national literature is determined by the ruling class and by its content. And I hope to have shown its characteristics in some decisive aspects as well as its political, social, and literary power.

In conclusion, I would like to say that my statements lead to the following aspects for research in children's literature:

Studies in the history of literature for children and young people can contribute to the history of mankind and of the social development of individual nations if they are carried out in conjunction with, rather than apart from, studies of the whole cultural development, that is, with the development of literature and science.

The history of literature for children and young people is characterized by the following aspects:

1. The historical and political aspect concerning its material, content, problems, and their social background.
2. The literary and sociological aspect concerning its form, content, and effect.
3. The artistic aspect expressed in its artistic and graphic design and format, especially that of the picture book.
4. The aspect of its relation to the history of science and its contribution to the progress of science, especially emphasized in the nonfiction book.
5. The educational aspect concerning the individual ideal of education, especially pursued in didactic and educational literature.
6. The psychological aspect concerning an attitude toward life instilled in the young person willing to accept guidance.

In summary: The book for children is, as a part of national literature, not any kind of literature but a specific field in itself. It is an especially important, yet difficult, field of literature because it directly projects into folk literature. The literary reception of children and young people is most closely connected with adult literature.

And, last but not least, some specific conclusions for library work: Library work with children in public libraries is extremely important because librarians work with actual children and contemporary literature. Care for the national history of children's literature and its scientific investigation is equally important.

The recording of the national children's book production is an essential and indispensable task of the national or state library of each country. But today this traditional form of recording the specific literature is no longer sufficient. In each country a center for scientific investigation and research of children's literature, embracing old and contemporary national children's literature, should be established. It should collect characteristic examples of international children's literature as well as secondary literature. International secondary literature is an indispensable research tool in this field.

In my opinion and by our experience the best place, the best location for such a research and material center is the national or state library. These universal comprehensive libraries have the best prerequisites for this task. One would hope that these libraries have the best "impartial" conditions due to their general character. If you recall the six different aspects of children's literature you will be aware that the concentration of national and international children's literature research in a special research library could foster too narrow a point of view: conceivably only the pedagogical, the artistic, or the psychological, etc., point of view could dominate the emphasis of research.

For that reason, the Deutsche Staatsbibliothek created a new department for books for children and young people in 1951. And I was extremely pleased to learn subsequently that under the direction of Virginia Haviland a similar special department for children's literature had been organized in your country, in the famous Library of Congress.

Let us hope that someday such centers for children's and young people's literature will exist in all countries and that they will cooperate closely. They could only benefit mankind, for honest children's books impress their readers deeply and for the rest of their lives.

Virginia Betancourt

Information: A Necessity for Survival

STRATEGIES FOR THE PROMOTION OF CHILDREN'S BOOKS IN A DEVELOPING COUNTRY

Virginia Betancourt

is the director of the Biblioteca Nacionale de Venezuela. She is internationally recognized for her leadership in developing a system of public library services in Venezuela with special attention to the needs of children and young adults. She was part of a small group of professionals who collaborated on projects such as a Book Bank of textbooks; a seminar on the selection, distribution and ultimate uses of school books in Venezuelan primary schools; a massive printing of a primer based on modern textbook standards; and the organization in Caracas of nine school libraries, a pedogogic library and a model public library for children and young people. Other projects included a staff training effort based on the conviction that universal education is essential if the people are to be incorporated into a nation's life and that education can be improved to help new generations break the vicious cycle of underdevelopment.

MOST OF THE ARBUTHNOT LECTURERS who have had the privilege of speaking to an American audience come from countries with a long-standing background of children's literature. They have presented subtle and interesting problems relating to their experiences. That which I will share with you will necessarily be of a very different nature.

In my country 50 percent of the population is not yet fifteen and the average publication of children's books is ten titles per year. Due to political turmoil, the population, until 1935, had not been exposed to a permanent flow of ideas through books. Our authoritarian heritage expresses itself not only politically, but also within families and other institutions. Knowledge, till now, has been used by a few to retain or gain power. The family pattern of the Latin-European countries prevails: male figures are predominant; decisions are made hierarchically; emotional ties are strong and lasting; and children are much valued, both as an investment and a source of entertainment and pride. Conversation is still the main source of communication, not only because of its frequency, but also because of its intensity and the high credibility assigned to a trusted personal source.

This is the situation in most of our Latin American countries. Those that have had a different pattern of development—Chile, Argentina, and Uruguay—are now under cruel dictatorships which consciously undermine universities, editorial production, and the circulation of books. Public schooling is available, but it is of such poor quality and rigidity that absenteeism and dropouts are frequent. This is true especially in rural areas and in city slums, whose residents constitute a high percentage of the population. Reading and writing are not essential for survival. In fact, books have been perceived to be instruments for domination by a powerful elite (e.g., the rich, the politically powerful, and the traditional church).

All this indicates that a substantial difference separates us from other countries that possess strong editorial houses with a full range of children's literature available in libraries and bookshops. Today, in Venezuela, we are trying to change this situation. We are searching for lasting ways to get books in the hands of a larger number of children in the country; for ways to attain a stable and increasing national production of books for children; and for ways to assist and encourage children to become selective and constant readers. It is a complex and, unfortunately, a long process which requires the support of political parties, government backing, and grass-roots recognition of the role of libraries in effecting change.

On this occasion, I would like to share with you two complementary and interdependent activities which we have developed and in which

---

Presented May 2, 1981, in Denton, Texas, by the Association for Library Service to Children in cooperation with Texas Woman's University, Denton, Texas.

we are currently engaged. The first is the organization of a network of public libraries throughout Venezuela where the accent is placed on service to children and youth, especially among the marginal population of cities.* The second is the production of children's books.

Basically, two agencies have promoted and channeled these activities (which are a joint effort of teachers, librarians, sociologists, psychologists, anthropologists, architects, journalists, lawyers, and many other professionals and technicians): the Book Bank, a private nonprofit association, which is the pioneer in this experiment in the evaluation of children's books, library services, and the production of children's books; and the Autonomous Institute of the National Library and Library Services, which is a new government agency with decentralized administration.

It must be stressed that private nonprofit organizations are uncommon in Latin America, especially in the controversial areas of education and book production. And the establishment by law in 1977 with backing from all political parties, of an Autonomous Institute at the highest hierarchical level is a sign of the recognition of the role of a national library system in national as well as individual development and the need to provide for its continuity as a basic community service.

In 1960, after our last ten-year dictatorship, a national mood arose which assigned an almost mystical role to education as the solution to both economic and political problems. As a response to this mood the Book Bank was organized and its first activity was to collect and exchange used textbooks. Through the experience it became obvious to us that the textbooks were of the poorest quality, that other reading material was needed but lacking, and that its distribution could not depend on sporadic volunteer activity. It was apparent that it was necessary to experiment with ways to create school and public library networks and, simultaneously, to evaluate systematically the reading materials available. The Book Bank organized, with government financial aid, Venezuela's first school library network in Ciudad Guayana (the most important industrialized area in the country) and the first public library network in Caracas. Both networks were planned and operated as demonstration projects. We now have twenty years of experience, from the early Book Bank demonstrations to today's services in public libraries throughout the country, provided by the Autonomous Institute of the National Library.

During these twenty years we have learned a great deal. Sometimes we adapted systems and procedures which existed in other countries to our needs. At other times, we developed our own techniques, often learning and making adjustments as the work progressed. I cannot describe for you here the details and changing circumstances of this learning process. I would, however, like to share some of the conclu-

*By "marginal population" we mean those persons, usually of rural origin, who arrive in large cities, cities that are unprepared to provide for their basic needs for housing, although employment is available.

sions as to the role of libraries in countries like Venezuela that we have reached during this work.

The first conclusion is that in countries such as ours, where there is no reading tradition, it is not sufficient to make a variety of materials of the proper quality available to the child or youth. It is also necessary to encourage young people to enjoy reading and to seek and use information to help solve their problems. That is why libraries cannot be just places for reading. They must also be centers of cultural and educational activity to which people must be enticed and where they must be won over to the realization of the pleasure and necessity of reading and information. A library cannot be a place of no character where an abstract service is given to anyone who needs it; it must be transformed into a lively place where materials are selected and activities are generated.

The second conclusion is that a library cannot simply be a place where information is transmitted. It must also be a center for the collection and organization of information. The information, which is already systematized in documents and books, is usually of a general nature, when contrasted with the real needs of each specific community. Nonetheless, in every community, there exist sources of information that complement that which is available in books and documents. For a child or a youth, the craftsman, the storekeeper, or the daily newspaper may be more informative than the textbook or the crafts manual to be found in the library. Therefore, the library must be an intermediary between the sources and the public. Both at a national and a local level libraries must assume the additional function of locating sources of information, organizing them, and making the information available to the community.

Third, we are persuaded that for libraries to become meaningful to people, a consistent effort should be made in the production of materials which correspond, in quality and in content, to the real needs of our country, particularly with regard to children's books.

As in the rest of Latin America, in Venezuela until three years ago, no publishing house produced books for children. The few children's books that had been published were the result of sporadic fancies of one or another institution, or, more often, individual efforts of authors who not only had to finance the printing of their books, but also had to peddle them from bookshop to bookshop, or door to door. This does not mean that there were no books for children on the market. We belong to the vast and varied Spanish-language community, and the books Venezuelan children read are those from Spain. As you know, Spain is a large book producer and Latin America is its greatest export market.

Problems of a different nature arise from this situation of a lack of indigenous production and the importation of books for our children. Some are evident immediately; others are only perceived with time.

We have a common language, but many idiomatic forms, and the words for certain objects and everyday actions, are very different in Latin America and in Spain. This presents difficulties, particularly for small children, and results in frequent stumbling blocks as they learn to read. For the children who are already set in their reading habits, this creates a vast gap between their everyday language and the language of books, a language which is and yet is not their own.

Until a few years ago, most Spanish children's books were unattractive because of their stereotyped illustrations. Their subjects were repetitious and showed little imagination, in the few instances in which original work was published. There were few reliable translations of traditional tales. Actually, there is a renaissance movement among some of the Spanish publishing houses. They are producing new material, some of it experimental, and translations of very good books which first appeared in France, the United States, Germany, and other countries.

But the essential problem arises from a larger phenomenon. References to cultural, social, and geographic realities in imported reading material have little in common with what Venezuelan children see, feel, and live daily. This creates a disassociation in their world view that works both ways: books deal with faraway people and lands, and their land and people are not subjects with which books deal. Thus, the gap between what is read and what is lived grows ever wider, especially for those whose life experience is limited, whose main communication is oral, and for whom reading is very difficult.

We, who work directly with children in libraries containing 95 percent imported books that speak of seasons, birds, and plants belonging to temperate climates and that consider the tropics and their people—that is to say, ourselves—exotic, feel a desperate need for books with more content of Latin American and Venezuelan origin. But we recognize the complex problems in production and distribution of such material in developing countries. The few countries with relatively well developed production of children's books, such as Cuba and Argentina, suffer from a very deficient distribution system and cannot compete with the Spanish imports. We are still linked to our mother country by stronger ties than those which exist between Venezuela and other Latin American countries.

The concern for being nearer our own reality, for knowing and accepting ourselves, is not limited to children's literature. Like any other country with a colonial heritage, we have a tendency, many times unconscious, to look outside our own frontiers in order to find models and norms—and this is true in all fields of activity. First, we looked to Spain, then to France. More recently, we have kept our eyes fixed on the United States. We are still going through a long process of liberating ourselves from the various tutelages imposed and accepted for centuries on economic, political, and cultural levels.

As Mary Ørvig said some years ago in her Arbuthnot Lecture, "Even if children's literature has remained for years in a kind of limbo, it is not an isolated phenomenon." It is not simply fortuitous that Latin America's first publishing house for children was organized in Venezuela soon after the nationalization of the iron and oil industries. A majority conscience arose which led us toward becoming the owners not only of our soil's riches, but also of our own cultural roots. It was a minimal portion of the vast income obtained by the Venezuelan state from its oil which made possible the financing of the first publishing house and the guarantee of a library market for children's books.

Recognition of a need to assert national identity by putting into print that which had been for so many years the patrimony of an oral tradition coincided with an accelerated process of urbanization. During the last twenty years, the rural-urban migration has transformed the principal cities of Venezuela, changing them from picturesque towns into large cities covered with high rises and surrounded by shantytowns—in Caracas, almost half of the population lives in marginal zones. This migration has contributed to the disintegration of the large traditional families and the loss, little by little, of the rites, the fiestas, the lullabies, the tales of ghosts which for years the old told and the young enjoyed. As a librarian who works in one of the Caracas *barrios* says, "It is easier for a child to sing a jingle heard on TV than to remember one of the children's songs which probably only twenty years ago his mother used to sing to amuse herself."

Television has become the favorite pastime of city children. Programs of low quality, many of them rejected in their countries of origin for this reason, are bought by the commercial channels—sometimes even by the government channel—and are transmitted during the hours set for children's programs. I daresay they constitute one of the few experiences common to all city children, who otherwise live in different worlds. The marginal children living in *barrios,* the middle-class children living in *apartamentos,* and the small group of the privileged living in *quintas* have different family lives, social relationships, and even school experiences.

In launching a national production of children's books we have had to cope with the obvious problems of any beginning enterprise in this field—lack of authors, illustrators, specialized editors, and clientele—as well as the competition of imported books, which are less expensive. We have had to concentrate on the revival of oral tradition in order to put it into print. We have had to evaluate the present contradictory and changing realities as themes for children's literature and prepare materials for a heterogeneous audience.

It is certainly understandable that some Latin American publishing houses, after a first stab at national production—contending with authors, illustrators, and print shops—have turned the page. They have decided it is simpler to choose, in Bologna or in Frankfurt, an interesting book by some famous author or illustrator, buy the rights for a Spanish edition, and print it in Italy or Spain. While this is a display of good business sense and there is no reason to criticize it, I think it is an effort which assists us only halfway in reaching our national goal. We need both high-quality national production *and* a good selection of translations of children's books.

After several months of planning and preparation, with the helpful and knowledgeable collaboration of Anne Pellowski, an American children's librarian with an international outlook, and with our eighteen years' experience in libraries, in 1978 the Book Bank launched its children's books publishing house: Ediciones Ekare.* There were no precedents for the editors, illustrators, or designers. Authors who had previously written for children had used, for the most part, pedagogic and moralizing styles and themes, and the books published were noticeably lacking in graphic coherence. But the books were useful as expressions of an initial concern for children's literature and they showed us errors which we would not repeat.

The first collection published was *Narraciones Indigenas (Indian Tales)*. They are tales of different Indian tribes which, since the time of the conquistadors, have penetrated deep into the Venezuelan territory to escape the domination of the white man. They are simple tales full of candor and charm, and they introduce children to old and forgotten roots. The individual books in the collection were prepared with great care and respect for the original versions, which had been collected by anthropologists, missionaries, and Indians. A preliminary selection of ten tales was made by the editors, who have extensive library experience. The tales were then read to children in libraries in Caracas and Guayana. The children made the final selections: *El Tigre y el Rayo, El Rabipelado Burlado,* and *El Cocuyo y la Mora*. The beautiful oral language was transformed into a written text which is equally attractive. This was a result of teamwork by the publishers, researchers, illustrators, and collection consultants. The illustrators went to the *Gran Sabana*—the Great Savannah, the plains in the far southern part of Venezuela—and also to the Guajira Indian country on the Venezuelan-Colombian border. They spoke with the people there, steeped themselves in their landscape and crafts, and sometimes suggested changes in the text in line with their experiences in the field.

The first tales on which we worked were those of the Pemon tribe. The Pemones live in the *Gran Sabana,* presently one of the regions designated as a key "development zone." There the most advanced techniques of steel making are being applied: Japanese, English, German, and Swedish companies and many multinationals, together with the Venezuelan state, are exploiting the rich beds of minerals and the hydroelectric energy of the great rivers. Far from this industrial maelstrom, but still in the same zone, the Pemones survive, clinging to their language and their culture. A Franciscan missionary, Brother Cesareo de Armellada, learned their language and was able to collect hundreds of the tales that the Pemones tell at nightfall in their musical language with ritual gestures.

The emotion of a first book just received from the printer was a unique experience. We had in our hands a book with a beautiful Venezuelan text which was also a beautiful object. It was good not only to read but also to see and touch.

A second collection of Venezuelan *Criollo* folktales appeared this year. It includes the favorites from the oral tradition that incorporate

---

**Ekare* is a Pemon Indian word meaning "the true message."

European, African, and indigenous elements. They are lively stories of rogues, tricks, and jokes—stories in which the weak but ingenious win over the strong and the brutal. There are tales collected by Pedro Rimales about *Tio Tigre y Tio Conejo (Uncle Tiger and Uncle Rabbit),* characters known in several Latin American countries under similar names.

Another collection, *This Is How We Live,* is a first attempt to present realistic subjects. The first title, *La Calle Es Libre (The Street Belongs to Everyone),* is concerned with the problems of overcrowded living conditions and lack of playgrounds in Caracas' barrios. The text was written by Carmen Diana Dearden, an anthropologist with more than fourteen years' library experience in the *barrios.* It is a direct text, bare of superfluous details, with dialogue drawn from conversations with children. It is very poetic in its description of the transformation of the humid hillsides, once covered with vegetation, into an accumulation of *ranchos* (shacks), sewers, and garbage. The illustrations were done by Monica Doppert, an excellent artist of German origin who lives in the lower part of one of these *barrios,* and therefore was able to show the essence of life there in each of the details of the illustrations and in the design.

The collection *Rimas & Adivinanzas (Rhymes & Quizzes)* was designed to bring the child nearer to the rhythm and beauty of our language and to help parents and teachers cope with the not always easy business of putting children in contact with poetry.

A small book in this collection, *Margarita,* is a picture book made from a poem by the famous Nicaraguan Ruben Dario. For a long time this was the favorite of Latin American mothers, who recited it to their daughters. The poem was forgotten, perhaps because its flowery language belonged to the beginning of the century and the image of the protagonist was that of a capricious, ill-bred girl. The extraordinary thing about this publication is that through its illustrations the text was given new life. All of its beauty was preserved, but Margarita was transformed from an old-fashioned princess to a courageous girl who decides to make her wishes and dreams come true. Illustrations show the palace of the king and his four hundred elephants on the shores of the Caribbean, and Margarita going up to the sky with scissors to cut a star and returning with a bright light in her bosom to a beach shaded by coconut palms.

In this search for ourselves in the past and in the present, in this effort to forget what is fashionable and to look back and see what is near us, we have encountered not only the interest of Venezuelans and Latin Americans, but also of other peoples. *Indian Tales* will be translated into Japanese, and another book has been found to be of interest to the Swedes, Norwegians, and Danes. In April 1981 at the Bologna Book Fair, the rights to *La Calle Es Libre* were bought by eleven countries.

Common interests with a Brazilian publishing house have been established. We have translated two of their books and they two of ours. The possibility for working together in Latin America is a really important and attractive one. We share a past and a territory, but we have lived in isolation from each other for centuries. The field of children's books is not an exception.

The complementary and interdependent strategies—development of meaningful library service and development of indigenous book production for children—must continue to be pursued in the years ahead. We have a long way to go before today's children (tomorrow's adults) truly consider reading a survival skill and believe, as we do, that libraries are an essential element in the growth of an emerging participative democratic society.

The development of community support is essential for the efforts that we are making to attain a real democratization of information through books and libraries which are still alien to our culture. We are still far from a collective recognition that knowledge kept in the hands of a few hinders cultural and economic development. We hope that the joint efforts of our library system and our editorial house, committed to political liberty and freedom of information, will make knowledge accessible to all and will make possible the real participation of our people in the definition of their own destiny and in the direction their collectivity will take.

Dorothy Butler

From Books to Buttons

REFLECTIONS FROM THE THIRTIES TO THE EIGHTIES

Dorothy Butler

is the author of *Babies Need Books* (U.S. edition: Atheneum, 1980) and *Cushla and Her Books* (U.S. edition: Horn Book, 1980). Butler lives in Auckland, New Zealand, where she manages a children's bookshop that developed out of her experience with children's books as a teacher and parent. Her use of books with a grandchild born with multiple disabilities led to a study for which she was awarded the Diploma in Education from the University of Auckland. She is the recipient of England's 1980 Eleanor Farjeon Award for distinguished services to children's books.

I WANT TO BEGIN by telling you that I feel proud and happy to be with you tonight, but disbelieving, too. When I think of the list of distinguished people who have preceded me on this platform, I am conscious of a sensation of apprehension, as well as wonder.

The bulky parcel containing the twelve May Hill Arbuthnot Honor Lectures given year by year since 1970 and thoughtfully provided by your committee, brought me long hours of fascinated reading, but did little to reassure me of my own fitness to follow. For I am, by nature, practical rather than scholarly. A tendency to fly into print has always been with me, certainly, but has characteristically involved declamation, rather than innovation. I am fond of trying to put things right, and have a noted tendency to magniloquence in a good cause.

Almost all of my adult life has been spent attending to the day-by-day needs of my own and other people's children. I am thankful that there was no one, twenty years ago, to persuade me that I was suffering from daily boredom, if not mental stagnation, and, in all likelihood, incubating a permanent neurosis. For those years seemed to me then as now, in retrospect, the richest of all so far and the most productive of insight. They were certainly the most generous with laughter and love.

One could scarcely expect them, nonetheless, to produce material of universal interest. That they did, in the event, give rise to convictions about the nature and needs of childhood which have become tenets of my faith, and produced as a bonus a field in which I have been able to work with conviction and satisfaction, was my good fortune. It is a field, of course, which is likely to endure. One does not run out of raw material, if one's work concerns children. The need for vigorous assertion of the rights of children to unencumbered growth—emotional and intellectual as well as physical—is likely to endure.

I believe that a society must be judged, ultimately, on two counts: the care it gives to its members in terms of their individual and differing needs, and its acceptance of its own responsibility to invest in the future. The latter, of course, means the preparation of its children for responsible adulthood, for the time when they in their turn will make decisions and establish patterns for future generations. A narrow preoccupation with material standards in the here-and-now must be disastrous for any society, in the long run. Examination of the national grant for services to children in most countries—from the provision of schools, hospitals and libraries, to parent support and education and the alleviation of family poverty—shows clearly the low regard in which children are held in Western societies, despite our claims to the contrary. And yet the child is, by definition, both unique and precious.

Each child reveals the infinite, astonishing variation of which the hu-

---

Presented May 6, 1982, in Orlando, Florida, by the Association for Library Service to Children in cooperation with the State Library of Florida, Florida Library Association, Florida State University School of Library Science, University of South Florida Graduate Department of Library, Media and Information Studies, and the Council for Florida Libraries.

man species is capable. Children offer, in abundance, the qualities the world needs, not only for survival, but for *triumphant* survival. Courage, honesty, initiative, energy, humour, an infinite capacity for love, loyalty, and forgiveness, and a fascination with the world itself and how it works. How to preserve these qualities? Teachers of eight-year-olds see some of them starting to slip away already on the wings of disillusionment. Teachers of fifteen-year-olds recognize with anguish that for many of their charges, the world has already assumed a grey pall, generated by apathy and lack of confidence; in many cases, hopelessness is not far away. These children have been deprived, in the true sense of the word. They have been robbed of their human capacities to love, to wonder, to laugh.

The letter which brought me the news of the Arbuthnot award sent me to my shelves for my copy of *Children and Books.* Noting that this well-worn volume (the third edition) had my name and the year 1965 inscribed on the fly-leaf, I recalled that this was the year in which I had begun my real involvement in the children's book world. For 1965 was the year in which I started a small bookselling operation from my own home. My eldest child was seventeen and my youngest five, and there were six in between. "Almost enough to constitute a sample," as a friend who was involved in educational research commented some years later.

Surely enough to make me feel that I had gleaned some notion of what children of all ages and types and both sexes liked to read; and certainly enough to guarantee regular help with some of the physical work involved in packing and stacking weighty boxes of books. This venture was meant to be a hobby, an extension of the unofficial advisory service I had been running for several years for parents—itself an offshoot of my involvement in the local play centre. Within a year or two, I told my husband and family, I should return to secondary school teaching, for which I had been trained. I am, of course, still a bookseller, and will always be so, while life and health last. I regard bookselling as a noble pursuit. Some way must be found to keep good and true bookselling alive, if the human race is to retain and strengthen its tenuous hold on sanity, its uncertain grasp on enquiry, its wavering concern with the significance of life itself.

I became a bookseller almost by accident, an element which, I realise, has characterised much that has happened to me during my life. A reasonably good education was mine as a working-class child through a series of fortunate chances, and my decision to train as a teacher, made for the simple reason that teachers in training were not only paid (however minimally) but encouraged to attend the university at state expense, was, in the event, a happy one. I proved to like the adolescent girls to whom I taught English; they were a mere few years younger than I, and, against the background of a rigid, academic institution, my fumbling attempts to relate to them and to meet some of their real needs through literature must have seemed liberal, however inept. In the event, they were very kind to me. I well remember flouting the syllabus, which consisted entirely of Victorian classics, and reading aloud, heart in mouth in case the head of department should catch me red-handed, Paul Gallico's

Snow Goose. That I later read *Winnie the Pooh* to the lowest stream was pushing my luck to a dangerous extreme. I should certainly have been drummed out, had this excess been discovered. The girls were, after all, thirteen and fourteen; but I had only recently made the acquaintance of Pooh and Eeyore and their circle myself, and I had been captivated. I could not have defended this dereliction of duty if challenged by the authorities at that stage, but I believe now that these episodes may have constituted the only real—perhaps even lasting—effects of my short teaching career on my pupils. For shortly, marriage and motherhood having claimed me, my attention was compulsorily claimed by a younger age group.

Several years ago, and somewhat late in life, I became an author; again, by the dictates of chance rather than plan. I had returned to the university as a part-time "mature student" as we coyly frame it in New Zealand, in order to remedy a deficiency in my background. I was ignorant, it seemed, about the reading process itself. Informed, as I believed I was, about books and their capacity to benefit children, I had no idea as to the nature of the reading task itself.

Indeed, I had never thought of reading as a difficult skill, any more than I had thought of walking or talking as unlikely to be acquired automatically by the developing child. Some people certainly walked, talked, or read with greater grace and skill than others, but these differences were of degree only. Basically, human beings *could* walk, talk, and read.

It seemed, however, that I was wrong. An astonishing but indubitable fact was claiming public attention. Significant numbers of children in our favoured and beautiful country could not read at an age by which one might reasonably suppose them to have acquired this ability. Reflection on my part produced only the suspicion that such children probably lacked appreciation of the nature of the task—its function, its rewards, and its significance to their own lives. Let it be seen that reading was fun, I told the audiences I addressed regularly, let children see you enjoying books and spending time with them, and all will be well. Increasingly, I sensed their doubt. My solutions were, or seemed to be, overly simple. My course was clear. I must return to the university and study, not the masterpieces of the English language and the lives and philosophies of their authors with which I had dallied all those years before, but revealed truths about the acquisition of reading skills. Simple, it seemed.

I emerged three years later, shaken but sustained. No one, it appeared, knew how reading skills were acquired or had more than a generalised idea of their exact nature.

I was justified in my own opinion—which had, as it happened, intensified with the passage of time and a closer examination of children in their schools, their homes, and the marketplaces of the electronic world. Fortified now with the jargon of the discipline, I might return to the fray. I must, of course, produce a thesis before the whole performance might be said to be over, but I had three years in which to accomplish this. Comfortingly, a friend with exalted qualifications in the field assured me that the only useful purpose of a Diploma in Education thesis was that of demonstrating to next year's candidates the necessary length of a Diploma in Education thesis. The few I examined had depressing titles like "Reading Miscues of Twenty Backward Nine-Year-Olds" and "Token Reinforcement of Disruptive Six-Year-Olds Using Metal Discs." I counted the words in these assiduously, and retreated with relief.

I will spare you the details of my anguished production (in the second half of the third year) of the thesis which later became the book *Cushla and Her Books.* Suffice to say that its accomplishment precipitated me, willy-nilly, into the world of authorship. The material, of course, was all there, collected since Cushla's birth nearly four years before by my daughter, Patricia Yeoman.

From chance teacher, to fortuitous bookseller, to unintentional author. The accidental element in my life has been a dominant one. But central to it all has been the written word: the book.

In my distant school days, education *meant* books. Our teachers, we believed, knew everything and it all came out of books. The passage of time, while it may have cast creeping doubt on the infallibility of our instructors, did nothing to lessen our faith in the written word. The way to wisdom, we knew, was through thicker and thicker books. The vital tool with which we must be equipped if we aspired to join the lofty ranks of the informed was the ability to read. Fortunately, the right to this sublime privilege had been conferred upon us by the Education Act of 1870, in faraway England (always known, in those days in New Zealand as "Home" or "The Old Country"). We knew, further, that whereas our parents had been obliged by circumstance and allowed by law to leave school at twelve years of age, we might, at the expense of the government, remain at school until our fourteenth birthday. Privilege indeed.

Classes were large in Depression New Zealand, and rules rigid. But children were children and we ranged from the quiet and conforming to the wild and insubordinate, with every shade of disposition between. One thing only we shared: a conviction, however unpalatable, that the game was to the literate, the match to the well read.

Some of us fell in love with books early, as children have through the ages, and I was one of the lucky ones. My seduction, however, had nothing to do with the pursuit of wisdom. It had to do, I suspect, with a mother who was daily seen to rise from the old kitchen sofa, book in hand, as we three children came through the door from school. "Goodness," she would say. "Is it really half-past three? I must put the kettle on!"

I was sent to school at five years of age, as New Zealand children are still. All four "Infant" classes sat in the same large room, in four ascending rows of desks. My brother, sixteen months older than I, was in the third row—"Primer Three"—and seemed God-like within these precincts—though earthy enough at home. Our teacher was elderly, with grey hair tied back in a bun. She was kind and extremely firm. And, wonder of wonders, she read to us, from a fat book called *The Adventures of Doctor Dolittle.* Each day at the same time she would indicate her intention of bestowing this indulgence upon us by taking down the book from a shelf and saying in a voice at once admonitory and full of promise, "Are you ready?" We were, immediately. Our hands were clasped on our desk lids, our feet (those that reached) together on the wooden crossbar at ground level, our lips sealed. That forty pairs of eyes glittered in anticipation I have no doubt.

I knew all about listening.

At home we were seldom read to, but my mother told us repeated tales of her childhood in the gold-mining town of Thames at the turn of the century. Her family had boasted, as well as the usual complement of children, cats, dogs, and horses, a monkey, and Jacko was our Pooh Bear, our Paddington. We often sat on after a meal, each of us requesting his or her favourite anecdote. There always seemed to be time in those days. "Tell us about the time Jacko took your red beret up onto the roof. . . ." Heads on arms between the empty plates, we would listen, our minds far away, seeing vividly the world of a small pinafored girl and her brothers and sister — making illicit toffee while Mother took her Sunday afternoon rest upstairs. (On one occasion small Emily plunged an enthusiastic finger into the boiling confection, opened her mouth to scream, and was snatched up by her eldest brother and rushed, his hand over her mouth, to the horses' trough at the bottom of the garden. Only when the little burned hand was completely immersed, was the large brotherly one removed!) How could we believe that anyone expected virtue and sobriety from us, in the face of this reassuring evidence of the spirit of the previous generation? And our grandfather had owned — and frequently fallen spectacularly *off* — a penny-farthing cycle!

Pictures in the mind . . . not on a flickering screen, nor even in a picture book. The best sort of all, for they have no boundaries. They may fade with time, but they never disappear entirely.

They are there, an inner landscape, a secure background for the absorption of later experience and impression.

At school, with the other five-year-olds, I encountered the Beacon readers. I remember shaking Book One with frustration, because the symbols would not translate themselves. And then suddenly — understanding! — and the heady joy of careering down the page, through the trials and triumphs of Chicken Licken and The Old Woman and Her Pig and on to the breath-catching adventures of Tom Thumb! I feel, to this day, that that first book, could I only take it in my hands again, would bring on the same old tingle. Promotion to "School Journals," issued monthly by the government in those days (one to each child), was a privilege to be savoured. My brother and I were in the same class by this time. (Reading then, as now, was the criterion for classification, and the amount of practice I got in evidently had its effect.) When it was suggested that we needed only one journal between us, I made my first impassioned public stand for equality. Ross was as firmly, if less volubly, certain that we needed one each; and one each we had.

Somewhere in the mid-thirties, an inspired editor published in the *New Zealand School Journal* that chapter from *Lorna Doone* in which John Ridd makes his hazardous climb up the waterfall to the Doone stronghold.

It is a great shame that editors can never know that, here and there, a particular child feasts for years, in his or her imagination, on a well-chosen extract; in my case hoping, without much faith, that the rest of the story would some day come to hand. It didn't, until I was almost grown-up, but it justified the years of waiting and became one of my favourite books. Wasn't I tortured by this wait, the uncertainty of the quest? Not a bit of it. Access to books was a hit-and-miss affair at the best of times; one thanked one's lucky stars that such snippets did appear, and seized whatever came to hand, gratefully. And one occasionally had a piece of *real* luck.

When I was ten, we moved house. The former occupants of our new house left behind them (joy of joys!) a copy of *The Prince and the Pauper.* I read it for the first time, knees under chin on the dusty floor among the packing cases. Parental pleas ultimately turning into threats, I reluctantly joined the work force. As the spotlight changed direction, I found another hiding place, treasured book in hand. We had no *Alice,* no *Wind in the Willows,* certainly no Nesbit, Stevenson, or Kipling; all of whose works must have been available somewhere in Auckland. But I learned to love language committed to paper, and it became one of the loves of my life.

Our home boasted that once-common shelf of "classics" which, I suspect, demonstrated a deep working-class respect for unattainable scholarship, once seen as the cure-all for poverty and ignorance. *David Copperfield* and *Westward Ho!* I read in a series of resolute sorties from a very early age, only half understanding, but determined to press on. I like to believe that something of the strength and structure of well-fashioned English seeped into my bones and remained. Several leather-bound volumes bore testimony to my mother's early "Excellence in Composition" (she finished school at twelve years of age!), and although the Shakespeare, with its postage-stamp print and unfamiliar format resisted my early assaults, I loved the supple feel and bookish smell of it and made sure it stayed with me. The Tennyson, miraculously, had firm, gilt-edged pages with clear print and romantic illustrations in colour. I quickly sorted the readable from the incomprehensible or boring, and the book became a standby in time of shortage. I did not care for *Pilgrim's Progress,* but read it through gritted teeth when—as often happened—supplies were exhausted.

A Bible appeared (I have it still) inscribed with the information that I had won it for committing to memory a record number of texts at the Gospel Hall Sunday School. I was a prodigious learner of texts. I loved them; especially those which promised doom and destruction to the wicked: "And the wrath of God was upon them, and they trembled!" Stern stuff.

The rolling epithets echoed in my head, and my blood chilled, deliciously.

Every Christmas brought its crop of comic "Annuals" of English origin—Comic Cuts, Puck, Crackers, Chatterbox (magic, never-to-be-forgotten names!)—to be stowed safely under the cushions of the old kitchen settee and hauled out for (how many?—countless!) rereadings as the year wore on. Today's children, many of them obliged to make do with the uncertain offerings of the TV screen, can have no inkling of the joys of repeated tappings of loved comic books. My brother and I read them aloud to one another interminably, laughing uproariously at the absurd bits, improvising wildly on established themes, and squabbling endlessly over "turns." Many of the contraptions we built in the backyard (and there was always at least one under construction) had their inspiration in these marvellous papers. And no one with a brain in his head would buy a comic that wasn't *packed* with print. Pictures were the icing on the cake, but the cake itself had to be solid with fruit! Someone gave my brother *The Coral Island* for his birthday, and I must have read it a dozen times between ten and twelve. And a girl at school brought me, volume by volume, *all* the Trazan stories. They belonged to her much older brother, and she was obliged to smuggle them out. Good friend that she was, she ran the gauntlet for me, right to the end of the series . . . and then started on *The Scarlet Pimpernel*!

In our family we were never made to "stop reading and go outside in the fresh air" (an order which had frustrated my mother constantly in her childhood), nor for that matter, required to come *in* until hunger, fatigue, or the elements obtruded. No one suggested that books were either good or bad, or that certain books were better than others, or that virtue or vice were attached to their perusal at any rate. In our cheerfully untidy home, one's loved reading material would certainly be "where you left it," even if temporarily submerged by *other* people's books and papers; and slabs of bread and jam, and apples, were always available for the properly associated activities of reading and chewing.

My own older children were part of the last generation in New Zealand to grow up against a background which had not been invaded by television; and the younger children enjoyed this same freedom because their home, along with many others in the sixties, did not own a television set. They made huts and dug holes in the backyard and gave concerts and magic shows and transformed the bush and stream beyond into a wonderland where anything could happen. And they read. Friday night was library night, and a highlight of the week. The books were a revelation to me. I had read, with fascination, the works of my countrywoman, Dorothy Neal White, and discovered to my amazement that there were books written especially for children which, in other countries, were reviewed or recommended. I realise now that, by later standards, books were still in short supply.

This fact, however, served only to encourage rereading of favourites; a discredited habit in these days of newer and bigger; but nourishing to the soul of those who practise it.

And modern children: what of them? They are born into a world which, even twenty-five years ago (let alone fifty), could not have been envisaged. Theirs is a world of visual and auditory impact, of instant impression. Flashing pictures and strident sounds take their attention from the beginning. Is it any wonder that reading to oneself may seem unattractive? Speed, children learn early, is the criterion for judging almost all processes. One's own rate of processing print into words, which must then be tied to images in the mind before meaning starts to emerge, will remain, without endless practice, too slow for one's own satisfaction.

And does observation of the world around children support the claim that reading is not only important but enjoyable? Their parents may *tell* them that reading is important, but the children's own observations reveal that adults use reading for very limited purposes; for enjoyment, they watch and listen. Small wonder that these children remain unimpressed by the propaganda of their elders. The evidence that books are *not* important may be overwhelming if they look around them.

The fact is, of course, that learning to read requires a delay of gratification, and this involves an ethic which is so unfashionable as to be unacceptable to many modern children.

A three-year-old can flick a switch which activates a television screen as easily as can an adult; as easily slump in front of the set and allow its products to pour over him. The effect is mesmeric. The brain slows down, if only because active involvement is impossible. How often does a small child, involved in a real-life situation, ask "Why" or "How" or ask to be shown, be allowed to touch, or to "have a try"? How often does the child who has just listened to a story ask for an explanation of an obscurity, request an immediate repetition—or rummage through the shelves for a loved favourite and say, "Now Mike Mulligan!" None of these reactions is available to the television viewer. Is it farfetched to suggest that questions which are bound to go unanswered will, sooner or later, cease to be asked? In an atmosphere in which the viewer contracts to watch only, may not the expectation of understanding in the end be replaced by a vacuous acceptance?

Small Victorians, expected to be "seen but not heard" in company, showed respect for their minds and bodies by escaping as soon as possible to backyard, street, or field. Their less-fortunate modern counterparts, seduced into a "seen but not heard" situation the effectiveness of which could never have been envisaged by the glaring papas and fluttering mamas of an earlier day, are subject to a tyranny which is robbing them of their childhood—under the very nose of a society which prides itself on the enlightened care it gives its children!

Away from the lighted screen, society organizes itself efficiently to keep children away from books. Electronic games and devices proliferate at a dazing rate. Knowledge and possession of such gadgetry have become status symbols. Pocket calculators prevent younger and younger children from acquiring the sort of simple computation skills which were once essential for the proper allocation of one's Saturday sixpence between gumdrops and a new pencil sharpener, with tuppence put aside for emergencies. Worst of all, one sees evidence of derision, even contempt, for simple processes, despite the fact that many of these were brilliantly conceived in their time. When I was a child, one could stand and watch a blacksmith shoe a horse and learn a great deal about a variety of materials and procedures; it all made sense. It was possible, moreover, for a child to ask a question about the process and receive an answer in terms he could follow. I remember the fascination of watching a serviceman repair the cash register in my father's shop. One could see how, when a key was pressed, a series of levers activated the correct number card, which promptly popped up into sight. And one could be shown where a cog had worn and caused the trouble. Today, electronic devices work, for the vast majority of the population, "like magic." Any sort of understanding is so far beyond most of us that we cannot even frame sensible questions, let alone expect to understand answers.

It is, of course, unrealistic to suggest a return to a way of life that is gone, but it is surely salutary to reflect on the child's view of the world in which we expect him, or her, to find a place, as we move on through the 1980s. It is likely, for example, that children will feel increasingly helpless in the face of technological advance. "They"—the inventors and providers of newer and better automatic devices—have all the power. One may as well shrug one's shoulders, press the button—and ring the experts when the thing breaks down.

It is ironic that the book, which has the unique capacity of admitting the reader as a contributing equal—a capacity quite alien to the flashing screen, which permits no active participation and, indeed, keeps soullessly on even if the viewer goes to sleep, has a heart attack, or goes away—may be seen by the modern child as an outmoded artifact. The irony here arises from the nature of the book itself. For in a world of almost daily change, the book remains unaltered. Examination of volumes produced by hand in English monasteries twelve and thirteen hundred years ago reveals the book exactly as we know it today: successive pages of text, held together by a spine on the left-hand side, and contained within stiffened covers. A triumph of design: only the invention of the wheel can compare with the development of the book in its impact on the history of humankind.

Significantly, even the detractors of the book have traditionally found no better way of propagating their predictions of its imminent demise, than of writing a book about it.

But books, alas, do not give off flashing lights, or emit enigmatic clickings. What is worse, something is expected of the person who would tap the book's resources. For reading is, to quote Pennell and Cusack (writing as long ago as 1924), "thinking under the stimulus of the printed page." And thinking makes demands. For the rewards of reading are *not* automatic; the reader who would profit from his contact with the book must "reach out to meet the author," in Martin Buber's terms. He must, as it were, take the text for his scenario and produce it on the stage of his own imagination, with resources furnished by his own experiences of life—and I borrow this notion from J. B. Kerfoot. The reader can do this, of course, only within the limits of his own mental and imaginative equipment; and herein lies the problem. The process involves active use of the mind and of the imagination, an investment of self which the reader must learn to make, initially, and continue to practise and refine if he is to read with real profit; to experience that steady and refreshing nourishment of the spirit which the truly responsive reader comes to expect. And there are further steps.

The reader must seek to grasp the meaning of an author whose presuppositions are different from his own, and also learn to avoid importing into the text ideas from outside, which were not intended by the author. There is considerable evidence that very large numbers of people, university graduates among them, cannot do these things; even a high level of intelligence and the ability to pass certain university examinations does not guarantee this level of maturity in reading.

How can we begin to develop it in children, and, even more urgently, how can we bring administrators—and educators, who are all too prone to see "learning to read" as an acquisition of skills, a black-and-white affair which debases reading to the level of simple computation—how can we bring to the attention of these authorities, who have so much power over children's lives, the urgent importance of the provision of the best and most imaginative literature, and the best and most informed teachers and librarians? For there is abundant evidence that committed reading is unparalleled in its capacity to develop the thinking processes: the capacity to consider, accept, reject, refine, and modify; that is the mark of the mature human being. We know that language is the key to human intelligence; that thought depends upon language, and that quality of thought depends upon quality of language. Over the last decade or so, research has shown that the process of learning to read—of engaging the mind with the printed symbol supported and sustained by the resources of the expanding mind—is of the utmost importance in the development of the intellect.

Even those educators who are not concerned with the benefits to a child's mind of imaginative fiction must surely be aware that interaction with the printed word is known to facilitate the sharpening of mental processes in a way not easily arranged by any other method. Why, then, do we find the appurtenances of reading—books and libraries—being denigrated or ignored by educational and governmental authorities in so many quarters, and time for reading, that most essential background for the development of reflective human beings, being eroded from their lives, on every front?

Increasingly, we hear of books being cast aside as inefficient vehicles for supplying students and others with the facts they need. "Education," we are assured by the supporters of bookless libraries, "is basically an information transfer process." Facts are what matter, it seems, and the most efficient way of turning up the relevant one is to press the right button. "Knowledge" as a word, has a formless, expansive feeling about it which is clearly unpalatable to the brisk programmers of fact dispensers. Wisdom is, of course, even more out of fashion. One has a sneaking suspicion that, as a word, it is on the way to becoming an obscenity. The concern of every scientist, poet, and philosopher from Socrates through Donne to Whitehead, wisdom is discovered in the 1980s not to matter after all. Wisdom takes time, and in the 1980s speed is all.

Humankind is a long-lived species which is likely to endure even longer if the accomplishments of medical scientists can combat the efforts of the destruction people. And the human young take longer to mature than the young of any other species. Is it not sensible to *use* this growing time? For children need time—time to reflect, digest, make connections, become aware. Time to experiment with things and ideas, to dream, to do nothing. Time to read.

Reading, as an accomplishment, is open to all children of average or near-average intelligence. One may equate it, in a general way, with learning to speak—or perhaps more precisely, with learning to listen with understanding. There is, of course, a strong internal push in all normal children to learn to speak and to understand the speech of others. Speech is the primary method of communication among human beings. The speech of others is present in the air around human babies from the time they first become aware (that is, from the moment of birth). The advantages of opting in to this two-way communication game are vividly demonstrated. The human child learns to speak "naturally," we say.

Unfortunately, this "inner push" cannot be assumed when it comes to reading. Where it does manifest itself (and it does, in both likely and unlikely situations, more often than many people realise), learning to read is often accomplished without any "teaching" at all.

But the average child must be persuaded to invest a degree of intellectual energy in the process of learning to read. And this persuasion, in our present world, is difficult to accomplish. It is not that children are born without energy of every sort. It is just that the game needs to be seen to be worth the candle. The modern child, surrounded as he is by diversions and amusements which arrive unbidden and assail him on all sides, is to be forgiven for not struggling with a skill which must not only be mastered, but refined, if it is to avail him anything. How can he know that the ultimate state—in which meaning pours from the page into the mind—is worth working for? How many people in the average child's life derive obvious pleasure from long, silent hours of immersion in books of solid print?

It would be more comfortable for us if the majority of these nonreading children came from "deprived" backgrounds. We must deny our consciences this salve, however. Cultural impoverishment is not uncommon in the homes of professional parents; and television, as a means of "keeping the kids quiet" may be just as commonly used by the academic parent who has "brought work home" as by the working-class parent who merely "wants a bit of peace." In addition, the child of professional or affluent parents may well suffer from a complaint which could not have flourished fifty years ago. He is probably overorganised and overtransported; he belongs to too many clubs and has too many lessons.

Before long, remedial reading must be sandwiched in somehow between piano and gymnastics, scouts and swimming. This child spends a considerable proportion of his waking hours being collected and delivered, like a package. What wonder that he slumps in front of the television when he finally reaches home? The adults in his life can give him possessions, services, and money, but seldom time. Both parents probably have demanding, or at least tiring, jobs. He may suspect, with some justification, that he represents an onerous responsibility in their lives. What has happened to his childhood—that time of exuberance, of wonder, of sudden laughter and irrepressible spirit? Does he ever lie and look at the sky? Little chance that he will have either time or energy to become a committed reader.

What then, is the answer?

My experience of parents leads me to believe that most of them want "the best" for their children. The problem is that many of them have no way of identifying "the best." They deserve, and I believe would accept, positive help; from schools and from the media. We have solved the problem of book shortage in most parts of the civilised world. It is time we faced the next problem: the shortage of readers.

As a working-class child in the 1930s, I was surrounded by children who could read, did read, but were always short of books. Now, as a middle-aged woman in the 1980s, I seem to be surrounded by children who cannot read, do not read, and are swamped by books. True, I meet most of these children through my involvement in a remedial reading programme. Of course, I know many children who read with relish and skill; but the fact remains that the proportion of children who cannot read is tragically high in all modern societies. And beyond the dense ranks of the "retarded" and "nonreaders," are the legions of "reluctant," those readers who, lacking the urge to practise acquired skills, fall further and further behind functional standards.

No one doubts that many millions of newly born children throughout the world will fail to learn to read, for reasons that do not relate to poverty or the lack of educational opportunity. If we think this matters, we must seek answers with increased determination. Are we to accept calmly that these children will inevitably become reading casualties? It is not enough to blame the schools, in my own country or, I suspect, in most others. For children cannot be "taught" to read; only helped to learn.

Reading is like swimming; we say that a youngster has learned to swim when he or she can flounder from one side of the pool to the other, using a combination of learned (or, if you prefer, "taught") techniques, energy, and determination.

"Good," we say, "She can swim now. No need to pay for any more lessons!" But we know that this child cannot swim well enough to save her life in an emergency; we count on practice to achieve this desirable standard. Mastering the technique was only the very necessary beginning—refinement of the skill is the learner's own responsibility. It must take place in his or her own time, away from the lessons which instilled the rudiments.

And so it is with reading. The difference between the twelve-year-old who is reading with fluency and enjoyment and the twelve-year-old who stumbles along at a seven-year-old level is all too often the difference between thousands of hours of increasingly smooth practice, and virtually none. It is our job—our duty—to ensure that this "practice" occurs. We must make time for it; we must see to it that our children experience early the unique pleasure that is to be had from books. We must recognize that listening with understanding is the natural forerunner of reading alone, and provide for a listening experience which will create its own demand.

And here I do not mean the passionless process which is sometimes called by teachers "listening for meaning"—and I certainly do not imply any allied "testing" torture! I mean the refinement of the human ear; the opportunity to experience the peculiar and pointed pleasure of the well-turned phrase, the excitement and stimulation of good and true English words used with skill by craftsmen.

How many adults (teachers among them!) still believe that reading aloud to children who "ought" to be reading to themselves will only increase their so-called laziness? Or that reading aloud to the seven-year-old who *is* launched is no longer necessary? These are the things to which we must address ourselves, if our children are to have rich and equal opportunities to become fluent, practising readers.

Simultaneously, and with vigour, we must confront those who would cut wild swaths through the body of children's books, rejecting some because they believe them to advance ideas which are in conflict with the ones *they* wish children to espouse, embracing others because they appear to recommend currently approved attitudes—and all with little or no regard to literary merit, or reference to the opinions of those who might advise. We are in danger, in the hands of these well-meaning but misguided evangelists, of banishing at least half the classics of the English language; in vain to protest that the real liberators of the world have always been the informed, the readers; that the burning of books has always been in the cause of human oppression.

The dictates of such critics, whether in the cause of antiracism, antisexism, or any other philosophy, denote an arrogance which may be excused as ignorance, but must not be tolerated. Good and true books engender true thought and feeling, and so allow children to think clearly and to feel deeply.

Such children will, in time, develop attitudes which reflect their increasingly clear and humane thought, making constant adjustments in their own views and conduct, and, ultimately, in the wider world. The best books reflect the thought of their times. The tragedies of past mistakes and cruel attitudes must not be kept from children if they are to be equipped to remedy the evils of the past. Of course we must reject stereotyping and prejudice in children's books. But stories which are flawed by such emphases are unlikely to demonstrate those qualities which an informed librarian or critic searches for in a book under consideration. Knowledge and understanding of children and books, and the way they interact, reassures here; but these are not, regrettably, qualities which are characteristic of these self-appointed guardians of youthful morality.

If the attacks of the underinformed are irking, the onslaughts of experts from adjacent—or remote—disciplines are intolerable. These are often casual fusillades fired with little thought and less sensitivity. Unfortunately, they are often given attention in the media which guarantees public attention, if not enraged outcry. The replies of the informed, being less sensational, are seldom heard, let alone heeded. As these detractors will no doubt continue to flourish and increase, recruiting supporters in all probability from the fields of nuclear physics and medicine next, we must gird our loins.

It is enough that reading itself is in danger of becoming outmoded; to have the body of children's literature eroded, and potential authors of quality frightened from the field, is unthinkable. Traditional modesty must be abandoned; we must say to these critics: "You have as little right to prescribe in this specialist field as we have in yours," and somehow convince the credulous public that our view is the valid one.

As I predicted when I began to write it, this has not been a scholarly paper. It has added nothing to the valuable body of criticism or information on the subject of children's literature, and has offered no real solution for the problems it has described. Its author has been shamelessly self-indulgent about her own long-ago childhood in a tiny country which only just (and not always) gets into the right-hand bottom corner of the maps of the world—and, in the end, could not resist the temptation to diverge into several different (but surely allied!) issues which irk her at the moment.

If I may assume your continuing patience, let me end with a plea: that we all commit ourselves to the business of giving our children back their childhoods; of going from this place with the fixed intention, each and every one of us, of helping the children in our charge—at home, in schools, and in libraries, as well as those unknown children we can all reach through our activities on committees, through our lecturing and our everyday voicing of opinions—of helping these children to *do*—to use their limbs, and their minds, and their voices.

And let us make sure that they know about reading and its capacity to give them wings, to lift them from the here-and-now to a place of wonder. It is surely the least we can do, who have brought them into the world William Butler Yeats had in mind when he wrote:

Come away, O human child!
To the waters and the wild
With a faery, hand in hand,
For the world's more full of weeping than
you can understand.

Leland B. Jacobs

Children and the Voices of Literature

Leland B. Jacobs

is professor emeritus of education, Teachers College, Columbia University. His long career as an educator began in a one-room schoolhouse. He is the co-author of *Using Literature with Young Children* (Teachers College Press, 1965) and *Ideas in Literature* (Merrill, 1966). His numerous books for children published between 1963 and 1976 include *Is Somewhere Always Far Away?* (Holt, 1967) and many volumes of poetry. In 1970, Jacobs was selected as a distinguished alumnus of the Ohio State University College of Education. He was elected to the International Reading Association Hall of Fame in 1979.

FIRST, LET ME SAY I knew May Hill Arbuthnot—not well but enough to have enjoyed her inquiring mind, her incisive speech, her delightful sense of humor, her commitment to getting children and books together. I admired and appreciated her knowledge about children's books and the ways she shared that knowledge through her speaking and writing. I admired her understanding of childhood as it came from research and her identification with children as individuals with interests and needs and unique identities. I was pleased that she came to her work of making literature vital in the life of children from being a teacher—a teacher who knew the joy of inducting the young into the domain of reading, that their imaginations might be stimulated by their contacts with the best their literature had to offer.

The publication of May Hill Arbuthnot's *Children and Books* was a landmark for all those who took seriously the critical consideration of the literary experience for girls and boys, and who recognized children's literature as a substantial part of the entire body of literature available to humankind. In this book she pushed forward critical thought about children's encounters with books judged to be of superior quality. She effectively laid a base in 1947 for those who today follow endeavors similar to hers. She laid a base from which to redefine, refine, modify, challenge, or refute her thinking about literary theory, literary judgements, and their practical applications.

May Hill Arbuthnot deserves being honored for her memorable contribution to the literary connections between children and books.

As noted in her preface to *Children and Books,* Mrs. Arbuthnot had both personally experienced and observed in the work of librarians and teachers that children could and would grow in appreciation and taste when happy, meaningful contacts with literature were provided them.

In the first chapter she observes that such happy, meaningful contacts are somehow related to human needs. She goes on to say that every child struggles to satisfy needs, and in doing so seeks to maintain "a precarious balance between personal happiness and social approval." The needs she sees as persistent and deep rooted are these: The need for security, material, emotional, and spiritual; the need to belong; the need to love and be loved; the need to achieve; to know; to play; the need for change; and for aesthetic satisfaction.

Mrs. Arbuthnot says that adults must also keep constantly in mind that "a book is a good book for children when they can enjoy it." If one puts these thoughts of Mrs. Arbuthnot together, one can, I believe, come to the conclusion that the voice of the author who is likely to attract an audience of children is a voice that has found a way to speak to what one might appropriately call "the authority of childhood."

Presented May 6, 1983, at the Center for the Study of Literature for Young People at the University of Georgia (Athens) as part of the center's fifteenth annual conference on children's literature in elementary education. The Arbuthnot Lecture is presented by the Association for Library Service to Children in cooperation with Scott, Foresman, Inc.

That authority of childhood, however deeply rooted in persistent needs, has, I would suggest, still other dimensions to be taken into account. It is important in the authority of being a child to wonder—to consider "what if," "could it be," to make room for marveling at what is known, for wide-eyed awe, for astonishment and surprise. Wonder is being open not only to what is possible but also what is improbable and what is impossible: What is behind the waterfall; what is beyond the wise-eyed boat; what is on the other side of the wardrobe; what is on beyond Zebra; or below the surface of the sea. Wonder can make the actual become uncommon; can make magic right before one's eyes; can make the mundane remarkable; can make wondering and pondering a way to the affairs of the world and a splendid celebration of "otherness."

Yet another important aspect of the authority of childhood is playfulness. Playfulness is recreatory in the best sense of the word. But it is more. It is putting in time—unhurried time for "trying out" and for experimenting to find out what something can and cannot be, can and cannot do. In this regard it is being unbusy at what many adults would consider to be unproductive maneuverings. Playfulness is trying on life roles that have not yet been one's own in actuality. It means "messing around" with materials, with language, with topsy-turvy thinking, and exploring the unusual possibilities of common objects. It means pursuing the search for reality in moods and modes that make the happening an end in itself. There is the much-quoted statement by authorities on child development that play is the work of childhood. Playfulness, then, would seem to be the means by which that work is done.

Another aspect of the authority of childhood can be described as "construction-reconstruction," which is not to be conceived as meaning only what relates to the physical being. It relates to the psychological, the intellectual, the social being as well. For throughout childhood girls and boys are discovering the logistics of managing their beings, their doings and knowings. They see that the ways of the world are carried out within accepted patterns of practices and rules and regulations. But they also discern that there are ways to take risks with such constraints. Thus they demonstrate their sensing that both rules and risks are necessary in their growing. They at least intuitively get the idea that no sooner is a conceptualization fixed than something new, something novel makes reconstruction necessary. Once they know what they know and know what they can do, children's active minds push and challenge them to do and know more. Thus children remake their worlds and remake themselves.

The authority of childhood to which the writer for children must respond, then, involves at least needs, wonder, playfulness, construction-reconstruction. It is an authority that frequently gets eroded by being bombarded by television fare; by being boxed into and tied down by controlled activities; by being discouraged from dreaming, musing, envisioning, imagining. It is an authority most likely to be kept alive by explorations and conquests of reality and by the delights of bidden and forbidden dreams. It is such an authority that children expect to recognize in the voices of those who write for them.

Authors' voices call to their audience of children from the past and from the present; in prose and in poetry; as realism, romance, or fancy. Some voices are gentle; some are strident. Some are substantial; some evanescent. Some are voices that will be transient, here only for the moment. Some are those whose words are so universally meaningful that they will be reaching children long after the person speaking to them can no longer speak. Some will be voices that make sense. Some will be utter nonsense. Some will be the voices of traditionalists; others will be experimentalists. But all that are those to which children will attend will, in some way, touch respondent chords in what girls and boys recognize as truly authoritative in terms of their experiences of being a child. And such voices are ones that put logic on hold and give full reign to aesthetic feeling—to imagination.

However one may choose to think about the author's voice in children's literature, it is axiomatic that that voice is present and will be heard. What's more, it is always an invitation to the reader to explore some aspects of life and living in the imagined world of literature. And what an imagined world it is—a world inhabited by street urchins and talking beasts, paupers and princesses; by monsters and mermaids; by treasure seekers and tricksters; by the baffled, the befuddled, the blinded, the befriended; and a whole host of individuals, families and peoples living side by side in a world that *is* though it never was, yet is wholly imaginable.

About this world that is but never was the author speaks to the reader directly and indirectly on the printed page. The author will tell the young reader precisely what the situation is; what is happening; what is being felt, seen, touched, heard; what is prized and abhorred, loved and hated. The writer will say this is the beginning, the middle, and the end of what is being read. The writer will make clear what the reader is to know and that is how it is to be.

Indirectly, and often unconsciously, the author's voice will reveal the substance of thought and feeling which undergirds what has been directly put into words. Though authors may seem not to be using their own voices in their works, they are never able completely to silence who they are, what they have experienced, what they accept as the givens of life, what they value, and what they believe. Though a writer may seem to be nowhere on a printed page, that writer is everywhere there, both directly and indirectly. The imagined universe created finds its landscapes, its days and seasons, its total cosmology deeply rooted in the author's lived world as well as in the created facts, feelings, and truths carried in the author's metaphorically fictional voice.

To succeed in reaching an audience of children, the author's fictional voice must come from a second self—one who, while living and working in Hanover, Pennsylvania, is telling about living in Borovia. Though the author may be managing a problem well in personal day-to-day living, a similar problem is going badly in the words that come from the pen. At unhappy moments in the affairs of one's household, happy, completely smooth-sailing times are taking shape in the writing. The young readers probably will never directly hear the voice of the person who has conceived and made readable what they are enjoying. But they know well the voice of the second self—that voice elucidating aspects of life and living which transport readers to places, times, and events never before so encountered or dreamed of being encountered. Yet somehow the writer's actual voice is present in the fictional voice. Somehow there has been a successful melding, or meshing, or harmonizing of what the author has lived and has said to be lived in the writing done. Authors seemingly have to speak out of two sides of the mouth: the concealed or "me" side and the exposed or "not me" side. Somehow the two selves become the medium and the creation to be read is the message.

From a different, but certainly not unrelated, stance one can think about the author's voice at what can be called the verbal level, the behavioral level, and the transcendent level of meaning. The voice at the possible verbal level is where the literary experience for the reader begins. This is what is said in the lines, the paragraphs, the whole of what appears word by word on the printed page. At this level the reader comes to know the literary news that remains news—that news in which life and its various manifestations stand still for the moment and for as long as this news is available to any reader. This is the level that holds the created world fixed and unchangeable so that readers, at their own paces, can ascertain such clues to images and imagery and perceptions as are needed to fully entertain and re-create what the author has actually written. Such clues in language signs and symbols, call forth the reader's recreation of persons, places and things; of objects scenes and happenings. Such clues encourage the arousal of the reader's reactions, emotions, and resonances. This is the basal level at which attention is caught and held in such ways that line after line will be read and page after page will be turned. This is the level at which the reader willingly foregoes other activities and goes where the author leads, or simply stops reading. This is the level that exists *in* the word.

The behavioral level, I would propose, is a more sophisticated level of meaning. This is the level that makes the author's manifestations of the created world so well-defined and so compelling in human actions and reactions that the reader believes what the author's voice is saying. Interestingly, when the human conditions are well conceived and well delineated, slight inconsistencies and implausibilities are passed over as fictionally acceptable, whereas one major blatantly false note destroys believability.

The behavioral level as voiced by the author deals with the rhythms, the connections, the interrelationships, the conflicts and their resolutions, the wishes and dreams common to the possible outer and inner life of a person—and, as presented by the writer, they have the ring of truth. While the verbal level engages the reader's attention, the behavioral level involves the reader. It lives *within* and *around* the words the author has employed.

The third level, and the one that lays deepest in the literary experience, I would call the transcendent level—the level that emanates from what one might describe as matters of morality and spirituality in one's living. In fact I would be tempted to call this level of possible meaning the moral and spiritual level were it not that it might be interpreted to mean the moralistic, which I certainly do not mean. For when writers directly moralize they are in the province of tract makers, no matter how much they try to conceal that they are discursively telling the reader what is right, what is wrong, what is acceptable, what, in sum, is morally and spiritually permissable according to their lights.

The transcendent level, which I think is definable, calls forth from the reading of a selection a pensive mood. There is, at this level, a challenge to a broadened or deepened view of something ethical or religious which has been taken for granted, or an illumination of what has been dark or hazy in one's considerations of the meaning of human existence. At the transcendent level, the child reader is called upon to consider not only the words and behavior in what is being read but also the essence of what has been written about. Indeed, books that touch the reader at this level leave a residue of meaning that lasts well beyond the moment of reading, beyond the memory of the specifics of the work. These are the voices that tend to encourage the reader to make more of what is said than is on the page. These are the voices of writers who make lasting impressions upon the reader, who bring forth for the reader an evocation of new dimensions of one's humanness and humanity. While the possible transcendent level of meaning is dependent on the word and what is within and around the word, it is *beyond* the word, present only because it is more than words.

From yet another focal point, one can consider the author's voice in terms of the language used. Since language is the medium of the literary text, it is crucial in children's responsiveness to what can and will be recreated and enjoyed by them. It will be crucial in the focusing of their thought and feeling. Of course no two experiences with a literary text will be approached or responded to with the same interest or expectations or intensity of attention. The reader's "activity of thought" and receptivity to aesthetic feeling being called up from the language used by the author are central in the meeting of minds between the reader and the writer. The various shadings of the author's language can and will serve as triggerings to girls' and boys' selections of images and sensations that are highlighted in their consciousness of what has been written. The author's voice, when free from incoherence and clutter, makes possible the interplay of what the writer has said and what the reader perceives to be what the writer has said. In other words, the reader hears, in the writer's voice, what that reader is able to hear, perhaps what that person wants to hear. At least, what is heard will be based on that reader's firsthand and vicarious experiences. What has been written will take form and meaning in the reader's mind because language has made that possible. The language of the text can provide routes and pathways to comprehension and deliberation. Language will have its part in generating the reader's responsiveness to the tone and content of the author's voice as comic, tragic, or ironic, and in the effects of the individual's feelings aroused.

When the author's voice appeals to the reader the literary connection has been made and the reading experience takes on its import. From the author's point of view, a sense of import is objectified in print, in the form and language used in the text. For the reader, import is a subjective recognition of significance in what the writer says in language and form.

Because this is the case, it is the reader who makes the text important in one way or another. Sometimes the import may be no more than the putting in of time, the whiling away of the moment. It will be a pleasurable but forgettable moment. At other times the import may be an escape from repetitive, routine activities or a means of avoiding what has to be done. Here the import may be that by having escaped for a while one can return with some degree of toleration to going about what has to be done. At still other times the import of the literary encounter may be the raising of one's spirits, the finding of refreshment in what others have proposed about the human condition. And in fewer but very memorable instances, the import is rooted in a splendid illumination of such abiding, life-long quests as love, belonging, recognition, acceptance. It is a residue of meaning that remains in a reader's consciousness with symbolic significance long after the initial reading has been done.

The import of the literary experience is, then, an engagement of minds, the mind of an author and the mind of a reader, made possible by language used to aesthetically order some components of existence. What the writer intends to do is not necessarily what is accomplished. In the end, the writer only does what the reader is capable of having done. The import is a transaction. It is a negotiation between two unique personalities, one who writes and one who reads. In this sense, import is always just a possibility—the possibility of an emergence of mutuality between the author's text and a given reader. When such a mutuality has been consummated, language has made it so.

In addition to and simultaneously with import on is the matter of the impact of the author's voice. Sometimes the impact will be slight; sometimes it will be strong. Whichever, the impact of the text will, in part, be derived from import. It will also derive from what is realistic, romantic, or fanciful as the approach the writer has used to reach an audience.

Despite what is sometimes thought, these approaches are not a choice between "believe" and "make-believe." Such a differentiation has no efficacy in considerations of the world of literature, for all literature must in some sense be believable. A prime test of a literary reading experience is suspension of one's disbelief. For such a suspension to happen in children's experiences with literature, the text read must square with what is of consequence in being a child. And what may seem inconsequential or trivial in adulthood can be life-size in the child's mind. It is, therefore, essential that the writer for children strive to make childhood fictionally believable. And the writer has available three choices of approach to an authentic, believable child world. Whether hilariously funny, or somewhat satirical, or serious and weighty, the writer will couch these aspects of life and living central in the literary creation as realism, romance, or fancy. One will quickly note that it isn't merely substance that makes the major difference. It is how the writer chooses to view that substance, and how the writer employs a given approach to substance as the best way to reach the intended audience.

When the author's voice is heard as realistic, the reader is called upon to deal with persons, times, places, objects, and events that might conceivably be from the actual world of the known and the knowable, the beautiful and the sordid, the commonplace and the extraordinary, the attainable and the defeating. When the author's voice is romantic, that voice, though based in what seems realistic, will expand well beyond the boundaries of realism to what is larger than life, what is adventurous in quite unlikely terms, what is nostalgic, idyllic, and certainly improbable. Too, there are the voices of fancy. These are the voices of invented lands, of imagined classes and categories of individuals and peoples, of magic and enchantments and all that is preternatural and supernatural. These are the voices that explore and proclaim all those appealing kinds of impossibilities.

What is more, each of these voices will be dependent on yet another choice, namely whether the voice will essentially be of comedy or tragedy. The voice of comedy is, of course, often a laughing voice. But it can also be the voice of celebration—of overcoming, of renewal, of transformation, of triumph. The voice of tragedy, or of the tragic moment, is one that tells of human vulnerability, of human frailty, of the loss of innocence, of victimization by circumstances, or of destruction and death.

All such matters directly affect the potential impact of the literary creation on the reader. While such aspects of the author's voice make impact possible by the very way the patterning is feelingfully ordered, these aspects are, for the most part, the *outside* of believability. They are the literary conventions, the structurings that have been used over and over again, and will continue to be used. As such, they are the means by which the reader recognizes ways to the text's substance and import, and thus the exterior of impact.

The author's voice with potential impact will not only sound well and flow well. It will, on the inside, present recognizable horizons and the feel of the authority of childhood which give the essence of the text something that makes the reader trust the author's way with words, and the author's judgement.

How many ways there are for the author's voice to try to reach into children's needs, their sense of wonder, their playfulness, their perpetual constructions-reconstructions of ideas, of opinions and judgements and reactions, of meanings, of feelings. How many ways there are for the writer's voice to make impelling and compelling what has been put into print. How many ways there are for authors to use their personal experiencing of the natural and the social world in order to give their fictional voices their particular believability, their authenticity, their integrity. How many ways there are for the author's voice to try to gain and hold a reader from the opening sentence to the last mark of punctuation.

Indeed, how many ways there are for the author's voices to speak to children. And how may ways there are for children to entertain the author's voices they decide to hear, and to enjoy re-creating what the author's voice has created. From yet another angle, how many ways there are for us who have taken on an intermediate role of bringing children and the voices of literature together, being neither children or authors.

There is no reason to be too modest about our intermediary roles. Actually, without us, what children would get the chance to know what an author's voice has to say? How would writers ever get what they have to say to boy and girl readers? We play a part not to be overlooked in a triangle situation that is always present when children's minds and the voices of literature are in the process of negotiating a reading experience.

For all who would assume an intermediary role, there is plenty to do:

- We can help children hear the voices of literature through storytelling and reading aloud, that the beauty of the word fitly spoken and feelingfully ordered becomes theirs.
- We can provide opportunities for children to become acquainted with many different voices—voices that span time, voices that approach human desires and quests in diverse circumstances and times and places, that speak in varied moods and tones and lengths, that meet such levels of children's interests as curiosities, concerns and commitments.
- We can preview literature old and new, that children may learn of the existence of authors' voices they might otherwise never know.
- We can introduce children to types of literary conventions commonly used to make literary texts intellectually available and intelligible to the young reader.

When, in the intermediary role, such things as these are done, the literature becomes available to children. In the intermediary role, one acquaints, familiarizes, shares, and encourages girls and boys to listen to many authors' voices, thus helping children, year after year, to broadened explorations in the realms of literature.

Besides using many ways to make literature accessible to the young, in an intermediary role one can do more—that more which relates to the transactional aspects of the reading experience. In this role one can get children on their way to competence as critics.

At first glance such a proposal may seem to be ascribing abilities to children that they cannot possibly have. However, when one considers the matter more closely one can point readily to the beginnings of criticism even in the very young. For instance, whenever a girl or boy continues to give attention to an author's voice (or stops listening to it), that child has assumed a critical stance with regard to that particular text. When a child makes clear that more of the writings of a given writer are sought, that child is making a critical literary statement. When children voluntarily offer comments about what is being listened to or read, they are being critics. When the young spontaneously recall something from a previous reading experience, a critical outlook on literature is in evidence. Or when children discover that certain literary structures and conventions, certain frameworks and shapes are being employed in the text at hand much as they have appeared in texts previously read, they are making yet another valuable critical judgement.

In the intermediary role one can listen and respond to all such evidences of criticism, taking into account, of course, the individual's age and backgrounds. One can make it clear to children that their reactions to what they read are important. One can invite children to do yet more communicating of their thoughts about what they are getting from their contacts with the voices of literature.

In the intermediary role one can foster the development of critical proficiencies by providing opportunities to review what has been entertained and enjoyed. Such activities as discussion, oral interpretative reading, dramatization, art products based on reading done, and the like call upon the child to review what has been read. To be reviewers, the children must put themselves in a relationship to the text different from the one realized in the reading act. Reviewing calls on the reader to reconsider what the text has brought to attention in the first place. The reader places what has been read in a new context, a context that insists on a selection of what is most appropriate for the medium now to be used, accompanied by reflection on the selection made. Thus the reviewing process contributes to children's development of competence as critics.

After one takes into account what has been said about children and the voices of literature by scholars in the fields of the theory of literature, of child development and learning theory and the teaching of reading, there remains this nagging thought: Ultimately it is pure magic that makes those funny little marks an author has put on the page become more than marks when a reader's brow wrinkles, when the head nods or shakes, when the page is turned. Something well beyond the stimuli of the reader's actual environment is holding and focusing attention and is transporting the young off the page to a reality that exists only in the mind. So I would propose that we consider seriously the disciplined discourse about this intriguing subject of children and the voices of literature—and then add, "But it's also magic."

Fritz Eichenberg

Bell, Book and Candle

Fritz Eichenberg

came to America in 1933 from Cologne, Germany, where his first wood engravings were illustrations for *Till Eulenspiegel, Gulliver's Travels* and *Crime and Punishment.* Eichenberg's visual autobiography *The Wood and the Graver* (Clarkson N. Potter, 1977) explores the multiple strands of his lifelong involvement in the book arts and the illustration of classic literature, in the creation of art on behalf of social justice and peace, and in satirical art. The Caldecott Honor Book *Ape in a Cape* (Harcourt, 1952) and *Dancing in the Moon* (Harcourt, 1956) are among his best known books for young children.

Preamble and Apology

I stand before you, a distinguished gathering of experts in children's literature, honored but bashful—and woefully underqualified.

If I have a claim to fame—whatever goes by that name—it must be due to my single-minded dedication to books and to my lifelong addiction to illustrate them—sometimes even daring to write them. And if you live long enough you produce a mountain—hoping it will not give birth to a mouse.

My other addiction is printmaking—preferably working on wood or stone—which enabled the odd characters I created to go out into the world and carry their messages into the minds and hearts of like-minded people ready to receive them. I hope that doesn't sound presumptuous but it helps to ease my conscience, egging me on to suffer for my convictions rather than enjoying the soothing solitude of my workshop.

Books have been my constant companions, in times good and bad. They have provided me with an education, with solace and inspiration—and incidentally with bread, and sometimes jam and butter for my family, a minor miracle. Books have also been my cake, and I ate it too, contrary to the old adage, without apparent physical discomfort.

It would be presumptuous of me to tell you what makes good reading for our children (of all ages)! May Arbuthnot has done this admirably for you and me! But I want to make a case for my position as a nonconformist, as most artists are anyhow! At my age I can still read with pleasure and profit *The Wind in the Willows.* That should prove a pleasant platform on which we all can meet, peacefully, or better still let's meet at Toad Hall!

I consider children as varied in intelligence, taste, and character as adults, and much easier to love and understand. Where and when do they enter adulthood? But then, where and when do we grown-ups achieve maturity, if ever? How do we preserve *our* innocence when the enchanting fairy tales of our youth turn into the brutal disenchantment of reality? Where, do we presume, is the dividing line that separates us from our children—the infamous generation gap?

As you see I have more questions than answers for you who care so much for and contribute so much to the quality and guidance of children's reading. Perhaps you can tell me why this careful nurturing of a tender young mind stops so abruptly once a generation reaches adolescence and adulthood, which doesn't necessarily mean maturity!

When we discuss reading, are we talking about words, and/or pictures? Are images not an "Esperanto" that crosses all language barriers dividing the peoples of this earth?

Whatever you expect of me, all I can tell you with the voice of experi-

---

Presented April 6, 1984, at the Minneapolis Public Library and Information Center. The Arbuthnot Lecture is sponsored by the Scott, Foresman Company in cooperation with the Association for Library Service to Children.

ence is the story of the magic, the mystery and the agony that makes an artist, a poet or a composer tightroping his or her way across the abyss of our technological jungle, hoping not to fall flat on their respective faces.

Word and Image

Contrary to the words of St. John, I believe that "In the Beginning Was the Image," and the man who made it inadvertently created the world's oldest profession, as the caves of Altamira prove. The images spoke their silent language long before Homosapiens became articulate.

Words are subject to semantics—that is their weakness. They can be interpreted in so many different ways—take the much abused *Love, Truth, Justice, Freedom*—even more apt to be misunderstood if translated into different languages and used by different ideologies. The image, no matter what the medium or the dimensions, visibly strikes at the heart of the matter. It is a confrontation face to face.

I am, of course, biased and expect to be doubted and questioned. Perhaps the artist has always been permitted to be somewhat naive and unrealistic, God's fool. But let me say, or brag, that in these many years my work has rarely been misunderstood or misinterpreted, and if it has, it must have been through a lack of clarity or insight on my part.

I can hardly offer a rational explanation for why I chose the above title for my talk. Looking back over a long life I can only affirm that the bell, the book and the candle seem to symbolize three mysterious elements that accompanied me on my winding path through life and found expression in my work: the book in the center, the bell and the candle providing the dramatic sound and lighting needed for my staging. Yes, I admit I am a theater buff and prefer drama to light comedy. I borrowed the title appropriately enough from the Bastard Plantagenet in *King John,* by William Shakespeare, who may have swiped it from some other more reverent source.

A Short Biography

Trying to dig up my roots, that familiar pastime, I discovered that the bells must have been ringing in my ears when I entered this world's almost brand-new twentieth century in the most Catholic city of Cologne, in the shadow of its venerable cathedral. It was the year when the bells were muffled in London as they carried Queen Victoria to her royal tomb, with all the crowned heads of Europe walking sedately behind her coffin. It was the year when the bells were ringing in Holy Russia, not to honor Tolstoy, her greatest writer and rebel, but to celebrate his excommunication for blasphemy. No bells were ringing in the young United States, but a shot rang out that killed President McKinley and made room for Teddy Roosevelt, the man with the Big Stick. Little did I know that it was the year when Chekhov wrote his *Three Sisters,* Thomas Mann the *Buddenbrooks,* the year that Professor Roentgen, the inventor of X-rays, received the Nobel prize, and Marconi sent his first wireless message across the ocean. I could not possibly have known for whom the bells were tolling in my native city of Cologne, but their awe-inspiring, booming voices have stayed with me ever since. After all, what inspires an artist but the disembodied voices that fill his universe, messages not bound by time and space, giving him extrasensory perceptions and insights? They often make him a rebel, rejected and misunderstood, or, as the rare case may be, hailed and venerated as one anointed, endowed with a mysterious vision and magic power to move people's hearts.

Assuming that by the nature of your calling you are all interested in storytelling, I dare to tell you the story of my life, abbreviated to be sure, but no fairy tale either. Not boring, I hope, because it reflects the single-mindedness of a creature who never wanted to be anything but an artist and a storyteller, always in love with the Book! A dreamer battling realities.

School Years

Unfortunately, I grew up in an authoritarian school system where corporal punishment was considered part of education, obedience taken for granted and no backtalk permitted. Art in any form was considered a hindrance, perhaps a nuisance. Music was confined to patriotic or romantic songs reserved for special occasions. What passed as poetry and literature served to eulogize allegiance to the State, its history and superiority above all the nations of the world. We learned by rote, and most of the poetry and songs I remember had to do with shedding your blood for the glory of Kaiser, König und Vaterland, or romantic interludes under the linden tree.

Even our physical exercises, which were supposed to build our bodies, were painfully reinforced with beatings and whippings if we could not live up to the standards of our sadistic instructor, a former top sergeant. My math teacher gave me nightmares. He hit me once over the head with a ruler and I learned to hate him and math too. If that didn't make me an artist, it made me a rebel.

It wasn't all bad, I hasten to say. We learned French and English well, on a strictly grammatical basis, and I learned by heart Schiller's lengthy poem "Das Lied von der Glocke" ("The Song of the Bell") which I can still recite—if provoked!

Struggling for eleven years through this grim institution left its mark on my tender mind. Four of these years were spent under the hardships and privations of the First World War, which made undersized little soldiers out of us. In all these years we studied only *German* history; Egyptian, Greek and Roman, "foreign" contributions to our culture, were ignored. The names and the works of Shakespeare and Cervantes, Dickens and Mark Twain, Pushkin and Tolstoy, to name a few of my later heroes, were unknown to us. We knew almost nothing of Goethe or Hölderlin nor were we shown great art of past and present. Giotto and Michelangelo were unfamiliar names, as were Mozart, Bach and Beethoven.

But these were ultimately the saviors of my soul. Our house was a haven of classical music. My sisters played the piano under the guidance of my mother who took care of my ailing father, ran our hat business, raised us three children with love and discipline, and took us to concerts, operas and the theater, when the war and our finances allowed. Sometimes I escaped to the zoo—I loved animals passionately—or to the circus whenever it came to town. We lived rather puritanically—a pet I was not allowed; it would have meant another member of the family to feed and take care of.

We had little to eat during the war years and our literary diet was meager, too, as seen in retrospect. We began, of course, with fairy tales by Grimm, Andersen, and Hauff, whom I liked best. For adventure we read Karl May, who described derring-do in foreign countries he had never seen. Old Shatterhand I will never forget—and I remember fondly *Lederstrumpf* or *Der Letzte der Mohikaner* [*Leatherstocking; The Last of the Mohicans*] by J. F. Cooper. Nature books were my great love: Bonsels' *Die Biene Maya* [*Maya the Bee*], Salten's *Bambi,* Brehm's *Tierkunde* [*Zoology*], Schilling's *Mit Blitzlicht und Büchse* [*With Photoflash and Rifle*]. These books lifted me out of my school prison and dropped me into nature, as far away as Süd-West Afrika, part of the Peaceable Kingdom I longed for. For comic relief we had, of course, our own home-grown Wilhelm Busch—*Max und Moritz*—the forerunner of the *Katzenjammer Kids,* and the endless procession of comic characters they spawned across the ocean which later my own children devoured in their comic books.

Meager fare, you might say looking back, reinforced only by the Lesezirkel, a weekly rental agency of popular picture magazines aimed at a motley audience of children and adults. *Die Gartenlaube, Daheim, Über Land und Meer, Der Gute Kamerad,* non-political, non-controversial magazines filled the literary gap every week in our family. They were passed on according to seniority and I, the youngest, was the last in the line.

But my hunger for books was unappeased—my curiosity for all the treasures withheld in school was growing and gnawing at my vitals. One day the big bell rang; I discovered the lending library, a private bookshop, actually, with vast shelves filled with books selected for an adult intellectual clientele. To me, it was a dream fulfilled, from rags to riches. I browsed with abandon, without any advice, no adult looking over my shoulder or beating me over the head. A new world opened up, a world of great thoughts, magnificent art, wit and humor and sheer entertainment. Exotic journeys into unexplored territory, and adventures on many levels of the mind were now possible.

It's difficult to describe to our more privileged youngsters the breathless delight of one so long deprived who plunged into this wealth of books. Each one was designed to give pleasure, excitement, food for thought, a chance to grow.

Of course I made mistakes in my innocence: I picked books by intuition; Nietzsche's *Zarathustra* next to Freiherrn von Schlict's *Militär Humoresken,* or Heinrich Mann's *Der Untertan* rubbing shoulders with Spyri's *Heidi;* Dumas' *Three Musketeers* standing next to Hermann Löns' nature stories. I didn't care as long as I was allowed, for a small rental fee, to take my treasures home and gorge myself on this forbidden fruit. I made up for lost time—I grew up fast, too fast perhaps—with the help of the book.

How I endured the last four years of school I don't quite know. My grades went from bad to worse—my last year I had to repeat. But then I graduated in the summer of 1918, with a diploma entitling me to serve in the army, for one year only—as "Einjährig-Freiwilliger."* Horrible thought, but then I was saved by the bell: The date is November 1918. A war lost, a revolution won. The field-grey army of the defeated stream back across the Rhine bridges. Somehow they look exuberant, with red armbands and flowers stuck in their gun barrels. *Nie WiederKrieg* (No More War) was the title of Hertha von Suttner's famous novel!

Our Kaiser, to whom we had sworn eternal loyalty, fled to Holland. The stifling school years behind me, I breathed for the first time the air of freedom. It was intoxicating!

I hardly knew where to turn first to catch up with all the missed opportunities, to learn, to enjoy life, to be an artist just turned seventeen!

I indulged in my love for books, without censorship; took my sketchbook to the zoo; got close to my beloved animals—now was the time to enjoy.

The lending library revealed more treasures: books on art I had never known to exist, Egyptian, Greek, Roman, the Fauves in France, the Blue Riders, the first Dada-Iconoclasts.

And to catch up on my reading, so long a closed door, I discovered all by myself the authors and books I had never heard of: Tolstoy and Dostoevsky, the French Voltaire's *Candide,* Balzac's *Contes Drolatiques,* Flaubert's *Madame Bovary*—the English Charles Dickens, Rudyard Kipling—a movable feast perhaps too rich for my famished soul but delicious nevertheless. What always seemed to strike my sympathetic nerve was the work of great writers preoccupied with the serious problems of life on this earth: social, political, psychological conflicts on every level of our society. I wanted to be able to deal with my own new-won freedom, to see these problems with the eye of an artist, an image maker, and to interpret them in my own way.

It seems far-fetched and perhaps ridiculous to compare the supreme world of books with the innocent Peaceable Kingdom of the animals, but both taught me all I know. Perhaps in my younger years I spent as much time with books as I spent with my sketchbook and my captive friends at the zoo. I shared with them their sadness and despair, but also their dignity, their resourcefulness, their longing for affection, their sense of fun, their devotion to their offspring. Had I not gone through some of their experiences in my own youthful life, perhaps with less patience and resilience? I came to know them well. I committed to my sketchbook and my memory my feathered and furred friends in every phase of action, repose and suppressed ferocity. How would they treat me if we met in freedom? I dreamed we would make friends easily.

Difficult times lay ahead of us in the wake of a wasteful war which had killed our childhood and almost destroyed our lives. As vulnerable as I was, I found my refuge in art. My education had not prepared me to use my own mind. Imagination and fantasy had been ruled subversive aber-

*One-year volunteer.

rations. Nonetheless, I was determined to join the ranks and the uncertain fate of the dreamers, the artists and writers whom I worshipped. I had begun to study not only their works, but also their lives. There were only a few who ended up with fame and fortune, admired and pampered by their contemporaries. I had chosen as my idols two artists whom I had first met in two books on satirical art given to me by a neighbor, a very enlightened priest and art historian who had taken an interest in my early artistic attempts. What insight Dr. Witte showed into my hidden ambitions to become an artist with a message! He introduced me to Daumier, who created 4,000 lithographs which reflected his countrymen, who spent half a year in prison for lampooning the monarchy, and who died half-blind and penniless; and Goya, the Spanish court painter and rebel, who left us the *Caprichos,* aquatints criticizing king, church and society, and *The Disasters of the War,* showing its surpassing cruelty. He died in exile, creative to the end, but deaf and lonely. I had chosen a vocation which promised few material rewards and had set my little ship in that direction, not quite prepared to face the adversities of an uncertain future.

Apprenticeship

First of all I wanted to make lithographs like Daumier's! I was accepted as an apprentice by the venerable firm of DuMont Schauberg, where I learned the fundamentals of lithography, rubbing tusche, grinding stones, getting coffee for my masters in return for kicks—secretly taking home small stones and making my first lithos—emulating Daumier! In the evenings I attended the local art school, improved my drawing in life classes (the first nude models), and studied people, among them officers of the occupation army, on whom I practiced my school English. After a year and a half of this regime I graduated to a paying job in the advertising studio of the big department store of Leonhard Tietz in Cologne. Good for my pocketbook, which enabled me to study the city's nightlife, but bad for my soul and my yearning to become an artist—another Goya or Daumier.

To assuage my deep depression, I browsed in my favorite bookstore and found, beside the picture novels of Frans Masereel, illustrated with powerful woodcuts breathing fire, a catalogue of the Academy of Graphic Arts in Leipzig. It showed, among other things, fascinating lithographs by Professor Steiner-Prag for Meyrinck's *The Golem,* a Czech Frankenstein haunting the streets of Prague. It struck me like lightning—I must go to Leipzig to study with the professor! But how to get there? There were no scholarships, no foundations—and my family certainly could not afford to support me. It was either nerve or despair that gave me the courage to walk into the lion's den, the office of the almighty owner of the department store, and ask him to send me to the Academy in Leipzig to complete my studies and take me back after two years as a more accomplished graphic artist. Herr Tietz looked at me in utter astonishment; he had never come across such impudence. He laughed heartily—I trembled—then he said, "Why not?"

Student Years

I became a master student of Steiner-Prag in Leipzig, the hub of the German book industry. I met a fellow student who was to become my wife some years later. I also fell in love with book illustration, an ardent affair which hasn't stopped yet. And then the infamous inflation struck, which reduced the mark first to pennies, and then to a scrap of paper overnight. Yes, we starved—and shared whatever we had. Not even my department store could keep step with the speed of the inflation. The monthly paycheck from Cologne dwindled to nothing on the way from one city to the other. But we were young and happy. We worked hard, and danced the nights away with a bottle of sour wine shared by a dozen classmates.

My first litho was dedicated to Dostoevsky. It was a picture of an exiled prisoner, his head half-shaven, an illustration meant to be used for *The House of the Dead,* which I illustrated sixty years later for the Limited Editions Club in New York. Talk about persistence! As a student I dreamed of holding my first bound book, produced by a legitimate publisher. The dream came true—with three projects I had worked on in my little studio under the eaves of the venerable Academy building. The first was *Till Eulenspiegel,* the lovable prankster and Flemish patriot who has always intrigued me, illustrated with my first wood engravings. It turned out to be a medium made for me and I have never abandoned it. The second book actually published was *Gulliver's Travels,* with twenty of my lithographs; the third was Dostoevsky's *Schuld und Sühne* (*Crime and Punishment*). Both books I was to illustrate again, a decade later and more maturely, in my new home, America.

The pay was miserable, the honorarium was miniscule but it emphasized the "honor." The money evaporated on the way from one pocket to the other, but the prestige was immeasurable—it boosted my ego and my status among my classmates.

Artist-Reporter

With three books under my belt—and no money—my marriage in 1925 changed the direction of my life and my ambitions. Prestige was not enough; I had to support my little family. I followed my wife to Berlin, the hub of the German cultural renaissance after the war, and I moved in on Ullstein, the large publishing empire, which covered everything printable, from newspapers and magazines to books. I got my foot in the door on the lowest level, a children's magazine, and worked my way into their newspapers and magazines as a roving artist-reporter. It gave me a name, a chance to be satirical (Daumier!) and, with a press card, access to the brilliant cultural life of the city, the focal point of the best in the arts, the theater, dance and music in the difficult post-war years.

Somehow books stayed out of my reach. I was known as a cartoonist with a promising future until I saw the shadow of a not-so-funny man with a little mustache (not Chaplin) falling across the dazzling city and darkening its lights. I was free to go where I wanted with my press credentials, and with little encouragement from my friends and publishers, I set out across the ocean to look for greener pastures. Green for hope, and for the freedom to express myself as I wanted.

The New World

The artists of the Mexican revolution drew me to Central America. After a three-month safari through Guatemala and Mexico, I landed in New York, made friends, and fell in love with it. The year was 1933. I sneaked back to Berlin, picked up my little family, and settled down in a charming old clapboard house in Spuyten Duyvil, within sight of the Hudson River, but without money and connections. "To spite the Devil" was not a misnomer—I had landed in the midst of the Great Depression. The unemployed sold apples on the streetcorners. I made my rounds with my meager portfolio, an unknown young artist with little to show that would be of interest to the American public, who had other things to worry about in November of 1933. What I knew of America had come from reputable, if unusual, American sources. In my publisher's office I had read and studied *The Saturday Evening Post,* the *New Yorker* (I could name every one of their cartoonists and illustrators), the magnificent *Vanity Fair,* the books and novels of Sinclair Lewis, Upton Sinclair, and Dos Passos' trilogy, *U.S.A.* Each reflected an exciting New World, with liberty for all who had something to say, no matter how critical. In Mexico the Taller Popular Grafica was in full bloom, and the names of Orozco, Rivera, Mendez, and Siquieros could be juxtaposed with the social protestors of the Old World, Masereel, Kollwitz, George Grosz, who would soon be silenced.

I had no illusions about streets paved with gold, or redskins lurking in the woods (Karl May and Fennimore Cooper notwithstanding), but I was eager to enter into the social and political life of my new and hospitable country. I had come in through the backdoor, uninvited, without recommendations; however, I intended to put my foot into this door—and keep it there—until the Big Depression lifted. We were surrounded by a phalanx of new friends, eager to help widen that crack in the door and push me lovingly in the right direction. Soon I was on the faculty of the New School for Social Research, headed by Alvin Johnson and Dean Clara Mayer, a haven for refugee teachers of practically everything from Spengler to socialism to Gestalt's theory. I conducted a class in wood engraving and illustration and gave talks on satirical art. I was introduced to the WPA Art Project, through which I did my first American prints—no strings attached—and soon found myself as a cartoonist for the ultra-liberal *Nation.* Each of these assignments netted me about twenty dollars a week, just enough to maintain my little family in Spuyten Duyvil, plus a lot of self-esteem. I can't remember that I ever worried about our Spartan life, I was well trained. At the urging of my kind new friends, I cut my first impressions of New York into my first woodblocks. My candle was lit, the books were waiting in the wings, the Liberty Bell was ringing especially for me!

Through the help of some loyal German friends I had been able to salvage some of my extensive library, mostly art reference and illustrated books, which turned our first American haven into a familiar home. Later my old workdesk arrived, now a veteran of six decades, which shows the scars and marks of all the work I have since done. Suzanne, my daughter, then two-and-one-half years old, turned my attention to the as yet unfamiliar world of children's books. I read to her with great pleasure Wanda Gag's *Gone is Gone* and *Millions of Cats,* all the Dr. Dolittles I could get, the *Winnie-the-Pooh* books and *The Wind in the Willows.* Later I read *Black Beauty* and *The Jungle Book* and more masculine fare I had illustrated to my son Tim, interspersed with Jack London and Mark Twain, in healthy doses.

First Books

How happy it made me to read to my children! How reluctant I was to give it up as they advanced in age and chose to read by themselves. Those were the days when I began to illustrate books mostly to please my children. My first, I believe, was *Uncle Remus* (Peter Pauper Press), then came *Dick Whittington* and *Puss in Boots* (which won a Fifty Best Books award), tiny and hand-set by Helen Gentry of Holiday House. A profusion of children's books came in 1936, not all worth mentioning, but they opened the door to my love affairs with librarians (chaste, of course), who discovered that this artist could also talk. I think the first to invite me was Frances Clarke Sayers of the imposing Public Library on Fifth Avenue in New York City, where I got a warm reception, so important for a new arrival. Inevitably there followed "chalk talks" in schools and libraries. I was mobbed by children and spoiled by librarians and teachers, and I loved it.

In the early 1950s, through my friend Margaret McElderry of Harcourt Brace, I produced my first perennial best-sellers: *Ape in a Cape* and *Dancing in the Moon*—still in print after 30 years. The first I dedicated to my son Tim, who often sneaked up to my studio to watch me work and criticize me; the other to Albert Einstein, the genius with a child's heart of wonder, then seventy-six years old, whom I had the great good fortune to watch at lunch, eating and smilingly turning the pages of my *Ape in a Cape,* which he loved. Talk about a generation gap!

But the Big Book, my dream book, was still slow in materializing. Dostoevsky's somber face was still looking at me from across my workdesk, reminding me of the visions I had had in my student days when I worked on *Schuld und Sühne* and *Das Totenhaus*—a far cry from *Ape in a Cape.*

My chance came when I met the legendary George Macy, who had started the Limited Editions Club and the Heritage Press at the height or the depth of the depression in 1929, a man of courage and in love with books—"beautiful, beautiful books" as his ads proclaimed.

He certainly showed courage when he commissioned me to illustrate *Crime and Punishment* with wood engravings, which, I believe, established me as the artist who knows and loves the Russian classics. I must have worked on the book for a year (who can adequately pay for an artist's devotion?) and it was warmly received in 1937. I realized how much I had learned in the intervening decade since I illustrated it as a student. Suffering is the best teacher—I could more easily identify with the rebellious student Raskolnikov. From then on, one challenging book followed the other: Turgenev, Pushkin, five Dostoevskys, four Tolstoys, interspersed with *Gulliver's Travels, Jane Eyre* and *Wuthering Heights, Tales of Poe, Stories by Wilkie Collins,* Goethe's *Reynard the Fox,* and Dylan Thomas' *Childhood in Wales*—for emotional relief from the heavy Russian fare. In between, there was always another children's book to keep me in touch with the young generation—*Mistress Masham's Repose* by T. H. White, and *Padre Porko* by Robert Davis were the most enjoyable for me.

It's difficult to explain why I always fall back on wood engraving. I have tried to cover this more fully in my monograph *The Wood and the Graver* (Clarkson N. Potter, 1977). In short, it's the mysterious counterplay between those two components as the title of the book indicates—the drama that develops in the emerging action—the light that spreads over the stage—the skill and intensity required to devote yourself with utter concentration to the development and relationships of the characters involved. The artist is caught in this excitement, and must succeed until the last stroke closes the circuit.

What Is Illustration?

What is illustration if the artist does not approach the written word and its author with great reverence? What is illustration is it doesn't add "lustre" to the book, enhance the written text, fulfill the expectations of the author as well as of the reader? Even if the author has long gone to his reward, as the saying goes, he is there and he looks over your shoulder. You have made friends with him, you have studied his life, reverently, often sadly; you have tried to slip under his skin, to fathom his intentions and motivations in order to do justice to the author's greatness.

By its misuse, *illustration* has become a bad word, cheapened by shoddy work in magazines and books. It's time to redeem it. Perhaps the fact that $11.8 million was paid recently for a twelfth-century gospel, 226 pages with 41 illuminations, will convince people of the ageless appeal and value of the illustrated book.

The medieval usage of the word *illumination* has always attracted and excited me. Monks, scribes and artists had the correct notion that their work was designed and intended to "illuminate" the page of written text, be it sacred or secular. Shedding light is implied in both *illustration* and *illumination.* The artist is closeted with the writer, the battle is joined and won on the printed page if the two form an alliance based on understanding. In the absence of these preconditions, it's better to leave *illustration* alone and let the word "illuminate" us without the help of an image. Some artists are, of course, singularly and happily able to combine their writing with their artistic abilities, but that is a rare gift. Most often there is a gap—one talent seems to prevail over the other; however, these rare multiple gifts succeed more happily and frequently in children's books. There are too many good examples existing to be ignored.

The Generation Gap

If I can't write like a Dostoevsky, I'll be his humble illustrator. My love for the great classics is an abiding one and I always wonder why we can't make more of them available to our children. It has been done usually in a bastardized version, some of the "meat" taken out, the text censored and "cleansed" to make it palatable to overly anxious parents and other guardians of children's reading.

I was first aware of that fact when I saw the nine-year-old daughter of friends of mine—in Hong Kong of all places—read Turgenev's *Fathers and Sons,* which I had illustrated. She seemed to love it. The parents had collected my Heritage books and assured me that Allison had read her way through them—with no damage done. She turned into one of the brightest Yale graduates I have ever met. The strict division between adult and children's literature has always seemed outmoded to me and prevented a useful and productive dialogue between the generations. Confined to my own experience, as an illustrator and a father of children familiar with my work, I would start with *Gulliver's Travels,* a rather sharp and colorful critique of Dean Swift's contemporary England. This delightful fantasy has been gutted and cleansed for children's reading beyond recognition. Why? Why can't Goethe's *Reynard the Fox* be presented to our children for what it was, a satire on a senseless intervention to restore the monarchy to France? The tales of E. A. Poe are pablum compared with the horrors shown to children on TV. How useful it would be to let our teenagers read Dostoevsky's *House of the Dead,* to show them how little has changed in Russia since the author was exiled to Siberia in 1849. What child would not enjoy Dylan Thomas' *A Child's Christmas in Wales* or Stephen St. Vincent Benét's *The Devil and Daniel Webster,* a New Hampshire man's successful fight with the Evil One.

Wherever I go I am confronted by people with copies of *Jane Eyre* and *Wuthering Heights,* by the Brontë sisters, asking for my signature as the illustrator who formed those images. They reassure me, almost tearfully, that they grew up with these books, which contain two blazing love stories and a fight for the rights of orphans and single women written more than a hundred years ago.

Why are we always so careful to keep books concerned with mankind's suffering away from our youngsters? They have to face problems earlier or later; joy and sorrow are not always mixed in equal parts. The Nuclear Cloud is hanging over their heads.

I know these books so intimately because I lived with them, impersonated them, and devoured them before turning words into images. Working my way through Shakespeare's *Tragedies* I thought: Is there anything in them that would shock a teenager familiar with present-day TV soap operas? Incidentally, reading them would improve a youngster's use of language! By the same token I would recommend selecting certain books by Dostoevsky, Turgenev, Gogol and Tolstoy uncensored for young readers. What powerful images are offered in *War and Peace, Resurrection,* and *Childhood, Boyhood, Youth,* Tolstoy's first book, or in Dostoevsky's *Brothers Karamazov, The Possessed,* or *The Idiot.*

When I illustrated them, I learned how to identify myself with their characters, saints and sinners alike. These experiences walk with you through life, they widen your horizon, give you new insights and compassion. Are these not also the qualities we try to convey to our children in the reading we select for them? Perhaps these random suggestions of a veteran lover of books and children may contribute to close the generation gap just a little, narrow it enough to jump over it, and exchange opinions with the experts, keeping up a dialogue between generations without the necessity of shouting across an abyss.

As for me, "doing a children's book" relieves the severity of my true vocation, and keeps up the dialogue with my children's children. T. W. White's *Mistress Masham's Repose* became a classic, as good things will if given time to mature, like good wine. How I enjoyed reading and illustrating it, as I did *The Two Magicians*—with John Langstaff's music—and even *Poor Troll,* which I did recently, translation and all, because it was one of the favorite and bewildering stories of my youth. It reveals the short span of human life in terms of the wilting beauties made of carrots which Rübezahl gave Princess Emma, his beloved one, to amuse and keep her—and then she left him anyhow!

For the artist, striving for perfection, in his work and in his soul, it is important to remain receptive to new encounters, new experiences, new insights—a sure way to avoid sclerosis of the soul. Teaching, at its best, means sharing your gifts and experiences with the younger generations. Searching with them for their creative potentials serves teacher as well as student. What better way to learn about the future of our society, of the world at large?

Art has its roots in the times in which it grows. Daumier's simple maxim by which he lived, "Il faut de son temps," always had a deep meaning for me. The ivory tower has long been abolished as the abode for the genius. The artist of our tumultuous time has the obligation to seek out the problems which confront society, be they soluble or not. If you live in a palazzo, you are likely to ignore the slums.

An Artist's Conscience

"The poor will always be with us"—that was Dorothy Day's dictum. For years I had admired her, the founder of *The Catholic Worker,* for her dedication to the poor and the injured (as Dostoevsky would have expressed it). I knew her eight-page paper, which consistently sold, and still sells, for a penny. Fate willed that we would meet at a Quaker conference at Pendle Hill, where she asked me point-blank: Would I work for her paper? She knew my work, she couldn't pay—I said yes—with all my heart. My first contribution, "Christ of the Breadline," which was my first impression of the Worker's House of Hospitality on Mott Street, appeared in 1949, and my work has hardly missed an issue in the following thirty-five years. It has been valued by hundreds and thousands of readers, illiterate or intellectual, and has raised the question: is it art—or propagation of the faith? Frankly, I don't care.

Though remaining a Quaker and an artist, I became a member of the *Catholic Worker* family, participating in their endless struggle to clothe and feed the poor, to shelter the homeless, to touch the untouchables, to fight for peace, to oppose war and violence, injustice and corruption, and to keep the faith! A big order, an unending battle. I am grateful for my modest part in their efforts and for my friendship with Dorothy Day, who described her life of trial, error, and triumph so splendidly in her autobiography, *The Long Loneliness,* which I was happy to illustrate. I learned from her, who loved beauty, art and music, and lived among the destitute in the slums of New York. We had much in common. She revered Gandhi, cherished the writings of Tolstoy and Dostoevsky, as she loved my illustrations for their books. Chance encounters which change our lives—don't we all wait for them? In 1952, Pendle Hill published my pamphlet *Art and Faith,* in which I tried to establish their interrelation. In 1955, I finished a portfolio of ten engravings of the old testament—most of them appeared in *The Catholic Worker* and many other denominational publications. My work would never be the same—I worked with a new zeal.

Stranger encounters happened on my various trips abroad, confirming my strong belief in the universal language of art. As a senior advisor to an exchange exhibition of graphics in 1963, arranged between the U.S. State Department and the Soviet Union, it was to me the fulfillment of a dream to see the enthusiastic reaction of the Russians to my work devoted to their great writers. We understood each other in ways our politicians had so dismally failed. Five years later I had the good fortune to travel through the width and breadth of Southeast Asia, from Bombay to Tokyo, to survey its graphic needs for the Rockefeller III Fund. I talked to thousands of artists and art students of a divided continent and found again a great eagerness and willingness to understand our pictorial language, our iconography, to find a common ground for art as a powerful cultural movement, enlightening, inspiring and civilizing, wherever it occurs.

In 1976, I was prepared to rewrite and illustrate the fables I had grown up with—known to most people as Aesop's and LaFontaine's. I wanted to relate them to our twentieth-century problems, give a twist to the old ones and invent a few new ones. They were published in book form under the title *Endangered Species* by Stemmer House. Many of them appeared independently in publications such as the *New York Times* and, I hope, lit a candle under the seat of some politicians. With similar expectations I tackled an old favorite of mine, much neglected in this country, *The Adventures of Simplicissimus* by Grimmelshausen, first published in 1669, a satirical novel of the trials and errors of war, specifically the Thirty Years War (which, it seems to me, is still going on—we just lost count!).

I realized another dream with *The Dance of Death* (Abbeville Press, 1983), a favorite theme for artists of the past seven centuries, with a set of my own prints and characters in contemporary costume, attached to a short history. Again, I hope these prints, dwelling on mankind's most enduring folly in its play with death, now with nuclear disaster—will go out into the world, and somehow—somewhere—ring a bell or light a candle before darkness descends on all of us.

I want to close with another dream, the dream of a man I revere.

Afterthoughts: *The Dream of a Ridiculous Man*

The Quakers, that small group of peacelovers whom I joined at the start of the Second World War, had a dream, Isaiah's Peaceable Kingdom. Though known as "practical" people, they saw the prophet's vision as a realizable goal, "beating swords into plowshares and making the ferocious lion lie down with the lamb," a little child leading them into a peaceful world (Isaiah 11).

Edward Hicks, the lone Quaker artist, not appreciated by his time and friends, was obsessed and inspired by this vision. He painted it countless times, not expecting approval by his brethren, but fortified by divine inspiration. The surviving paintings are now the prized possessions of art collectors all over the country—an artist's impossible dream come true.

Many years ago I felt compelled to follow Hick's and Isaiah's lead. I cut various versions of the Peaceable Kingdom, as I saw it, to send to my friends at Christmastime. They were used and reproduced subsequently by many publications, and no one has yet argued with me that the lion and the wolf would never eat straw if they could sink their fangs into a juicy lamb chop.

I am encouraged and stubborn enough to continue to dream up different interpretations of Isaiah's vision—a dove turning tables on a hawk, St. Francis preaching to the wolves, a Peaceable Kingdom on the moon—the pictorial possibilities are endless although I am not much of an optimist as to their effectiveness. In fact, I am fully aware that I am engaged in a quixotic mission—I do read the papers and listen to the news! But I take courage from an appeal made by Dostoevsky a few years before he died. I excerpted it from the last chapter of his *Dream of a Ridiculous Man:*

> And what about our life? Is that not a dream too? Even if there never is a Heaven on Earth, even then I shall go on preaching . . . how simple it all is: in one day, in one hour, everything could be changed at once! *The main thing is to love your neighbor as yourself* . . . that is everything, nothing else matters.

If we could only teach our children this lesson, they could lead us into the Peaceable Kingdom! Feodor, do you hear me? May we join you? Perhaps one day, before it's too late, the world may be listening to us.

Patricia Wrightson

Stones into Pools

Patricia Wrightson

is the author of fiction books published for children, including *A Racecourse for Andy* (U.S. edition: Harcourt, 1968) and *The Dark Bright Water* (U.S. edition: Atheneum, 1979). Many of her books are ALA Notable Children's Books. She is a four-time recipient of the Book of the Year Award from the Children's Book Council of Australia: in 1956 for *The Crooked Snake* (Angus & Robertson, 1955); in 1974 for *The Nargun and the Stars* (U.S. edition: Atheneum, 1974); in 1978 for *The Ice Is Coming* (U.S. edition: Atheneum, 1977); and in 1984 for *A Little Fear* (U.S. edition: Atheneum, 1983). In 1986, the International Board on Books for Young People awarded Wrightson the Hans Christian Andersen Medal, the international recognition of an author's works as an outstanding achievement in the field of children's literature. Wrightson lives near Sydney, in New South Wales, Australia.

On that exciting day when I was invited to deliver the May Hill Arbuthnot Honor Lecture, I at once went into a state of panic. That was quite usual, only perhaps more justified than usual. The organizers were kind enough to send me copies of previous papers in the series: it didn't help. They were all by notable people, qualified people, whose long experience was built on a sound base of study; people who knew what they did and why they did it.

I'm not one of those. I'm not really sure what I do or why I do it. So you must accept that I can speak only from my experience, and that what is true for me may not be true for anyone else, and even that I may be discovering it as I go along.

I probably would have been better for a college course in writing—but, true to my empiricism and my native obstinacy, I don't really believe that writing *can* be taught. I know it is taught, commonly in your country and increasingly in mine; I've even been called on now and then to teach it. Yet I can't be convinced that it can or should be taught.

I once laboured to convince a lady, an earnest student of Australian folklore, that she should not send an Aboriginal hairy-man aloft in a flying teapot, since teapots are outside the world of hairy-men, and anyway the species can fly without them. This lady tried—a little bit— to have a proper regard for authenticity and conviction, but it was that teapot that had set her fingers itching for a pen. At last I saw that I was the one who was being unreasonable; it was her story and she had to tell it her way. She was herself; she couldn't become another writer. Deprived of her teapot she could only make guided choices from a set of stereotypes. With it, there was still the chance that she might be lifted on a wave of conviction strong enough to carry her readers with her. It was the chance she had to take; the chance that every writer has to take.

Is there a right way to tell a story? Surely there is: a different one for every writer. And just as surely, this is what gives life and strength to literature. The same stories are told and retold and told again, and still they're fresh and different and alive: as alive and different and fresh as their authors, who are as different, fresh and alive as other people. Every writer has to discover the inner vision, as well as the techniques, that are secretly and only his. You find them by needing them: when you're wholly engrossed in a story, urgently trying to grasp and shape and convey it. Writing teaches writing.

I remember a day, a long time ago, when I was working on a story called "The Feather Star." Vaguely, through an open window, I half-heard my father calling, but of course I went on working. In another moment he irrupted into my room: I registered a faint impression of, "Ejaculation! Tut-mutter!" As he seized the blazing waste-paper basket at my feet and rushed away, I surfaced just enough to chuckle at my

---

Presented April 16, 1985, at Indiana University, hosted by the Stone Hills Area Library Services Authority, Bloomington, Indiana. The 1985 Arbuthnot Lecture is sponsored by the Scott, Foresman Company and Margaret K. McElderry Books in cooperation with the Association for Library Service to Children.

own absurdity. That dealt with, I didn't see my father at all when he came back to open doors and get rid of the volumes of smoke. It's when you're too engrossed to notice that the room is on fire that you discover how to handle a story.

But probably I'm being unfair to the college course and they don't really aim to teach the skill of achieving publication. That would be more valid, for publication matters acutely, and writers may need to learn it since it's a separate skill. In fact, at the deep-down level at which I find myself thinking, publication has nothing at all to do with writing.

Editors and royalties and up-front payments; reviews and critical studies and literary values; libraries and audiovisual and reluctant readers; all of these are important, matter acutely, and yet are quite irrelevant. They're the complex superstructure that we've built around the skills of writing. Writers may need to work within this superstructure, but I don't believe they work for it.

Let the superstructure collapse, and writers will go on writing. Allow them a personal happy-ending of fame and fortune, and they'll thank you warmly and go on writing. Assure them of immortality, promise them that their names are now preserved for all time, and they'll thank you warmly and go on writing. As they learn from story, so they're slaves to story. Practical purposes can be achieved, but the old, simple-minded motive can never be satisfied: the motive of story itself.

Even today, in spite of the complex structure of which this meeting is a part, I don't believe many stories are written for reputation or royalties, for reviews or posterity, or even for children. They're written for a stranger, for Someone Out There: that rare, unknown precious soul who will respond. Given one warm and seeing response from somewhere in the world, a writer standing in the dole queue will glow with success. Publication may serve its hundred useful purposes for society; to the writer it's the way to reach the stranger.

But even when you've reached them, responsive strangers are often shy. They don't often write to give you their response; and there's no longer a circle of faces round the fire, faces rapt or restless, to let you see the power of the story. As for letters, people write to ask for information and advice; children spurred on by teachers write to ask questions and display your reply; but only a handful write to say, "I loved it. I felt . . . I thought . . ." And that, I promise you, is the real reason why reviewers were invented. They may serve a dozen useful purposes for society; to the writer they are faces round the fire.

We have grown accustomed, you see, to thinking in terms of books and literature; and so we sometimes get the emphasis wrong. Books are simply a packaging of story. Literature exists on the authority of story and not the other way around. You don't need to examine a story to see whether it measures up to literature—though you may need to examine literature to see whether it measures up to story—for every story exists in its own right. If you don't like it, better read something else; this story wasn't written for you but for some other stranger. Story is something much larger, more fundamental, more invincible, than books or literature.

It may be solemn or poetic or the purest fun, but it's always something nore. It's a system of thought for exploring life in terms of circum-tances and people; a system that proposes by example, and defines and lluminates by demonstration. But its particular skill, as well as its par-icular power, lies in its directness of communication: it's a system of hinking directly into someone else's mind. It conveys not an argument lrawn from experience but the experience itself, illuminated; it is a di-ect extension of my life and thought and experience to you and yours to ne. Story is communication so finely tuned that is sounds like silence.

Because it thinks always about life and people in a framework of cir-umstance, its conclusions are not mathmatically final, to be ruled off eatly like a sum. They always lead on: back into life, on into fresh hought and new conclusions. So story moves on with life itself, and the ame story may be relevant in new ways at new times; a tale that ex-lored the concept of the sun as a burning chariot travelling over the sky nay be relevant in the age of radio-telescopes for its illumination of fear r vanity, and of man's own questioning habits of thought.

Story explores the intangible as science can't do, defining through ex-erience what can't be defined in words. It explores the unknown, spec-lating in human terms. It extends not only mind to mind but mind it-elf, teaching it the freedom to explore and the power to see what isn't here; and this is a power that can't be taught by visual means. If we uild around it a complexity that, for any reason, fences any child off om story, we do well to worry: we have cut that child off from the think-ıg, the defining, the shared experience, of its kind. Story is a mark of Ían.

So now, perhaps, if you wanted to know what it is that writers do I ight answer, in my wrong-headed way, that they drop stones into ools: finding a visionary stone, handling and weighing it; dropping it ıto a pool of another mind; watching for the ripples to spread, and per-aps for the stirred water to give something back. And if you asked why ıey do it I might answer that everyone shares in story, but writers hap-en, some of the time, to be on the transmitting rather than the receiving nd. They are just a few accidental words of the book itself in all its rms: painted in caves, impressed into clay, penned on papyrus, spo-en by firelight, or fingered into a word-processor.

The novel is a modern invention—if you ignore, for instance, the *bu-aram*: long traditional tales with songs interspersed, that were contin-ed over several nights in the camps of some of the Australian Aborig-es. They were not ritual stories. They were told and sung for ıtertainment and for literature; just as my father would read us, say, *avid Copperfield* night after night before bed. The *budaram* were still be-g told and sung within recent memory, yet they could be twice as old as papyrus scroll.

There are even older Australian stories still alive. Some of them tell of e time when our deserts were lush and green, some of extinct giant ıimals whose bones have indeed been found among bones of the peo-e. The current estimate is that the Aborigines have occupied Australia r something like forty-thousand years: almost halfway back to Neanderthal Man. This is no reliable dating of the stories, of course, but we don't need that to establish the age of story. For Neanderthal Man himself, one-hundred-thousand years ago, buried his dead with ceremony, and it is not humanly possible to believe that he did it in silence. He must have conveyed, at least to each generation, the story of why, and in what manner. Story begins when man begins, and flows forward with him out of the ages.

We haven't long been aware of this river of continuity: of life and experience flowing down to us out of the whole country of mankind. Until lately we thought of continuity in terms of Greece and Rome. Only since the Brothers Grimm and folklore, since the finding and decoding of Ancient Egypt and Sumeria, have we had a longer view. Now we know that if you could look back all that long, dark way through the ages, right back to the painted caves, the whole way would be lined with human figures slumped in thought and struggling to convey: fingering and weighing their visionary stones, judging how to drop or slip them into the pools of other minds, wondering if the minds would stir and the ripples spread.

I'm certainly no student, either of folklore or of archaeology. I've read only a little, for my own purposes, and I read always like a writer: in terms of life, circumstance and humanity. And what this reading has given me is, more than anything else, a warm sense of familiarity, of recognition, of experience passed on from Man to men. A sense of mankind seen whole.

I remember reading a biologist's comment that if some alien creature could visit this planet, it would be astonished at the distance we set between man and mouse. To an alien the differences would appear so slight, and the similarities so great, it would be clear that a man and a mouse were close relatives. So what, I wonder, would this visitor think of the distance we have set between man and man? The alien would go away laughing, to tell the crazy joke to all the galaxy.

For here is the record revealed, and the differences are swallowed up in the sameness. Here are school exercises, careful sentences impressed in clay, painted on shards, and pencilled along pale-blue lines in an exercise-book. Here is a code of law set down four thousand years ago and old even then; we never saw it till lately, but its ripples have spread forward into our own laws. Here is a nation's heroicised view of itself, successful man's self-satisfaction, a love-song, a law-suit, a traveller's tale, a list of taxes; all ancient, long-forgotten, and relevant and modern. And here is story exploring life, the known and unknown and the intangible: proposing and testing and defining by the same system; conveying with the same power directly into other minds, reaching conclusions that lead back into life and on into new thought. Dropping stones into pools.

And the ripples reached us even when we didn't see them. You and as persons may often be in doubt or disagree; we may hotly debate terms, or means, or applications. As a kind we are not in doubt; we know our values and purposes. We have shared in the experience of mankind.

"No man is an island; pride is arid; personal power is a dangerous evil." Modern maxims proved by recent history, themes for a hundred modern novels—but they reached us long ago in the ripples of old stories. Unspoken, they came to us in tales of great hunters rescued by tiny beasts, of proud princesses and swineherds, of the dangerous evil of witches. "Simple goodwill is worth more than a devious mind"; a hundred triumphant simpletons have shown it. "The greatest beauty is kindness"; dozens of cruel stepmothers, though they worked through magic, have proved the point in terms of life and humanity. These are our foundation-values, often rethought, retested, re-explored, but never questioned. We don't question them because we have not merely learnt them; we have directly shared the experience of them in story.

These were the stories of simple people, whose journeys were short and made on foot over muddy forest tracks; for whom a neighborhood was a world, and even natural science was generally magic. Life for us, materially, could hardly be more different; yet what comes through is sameness, a brotherhood in life. Those early people thought by our system and passed it on to us. They had no glimpse of our century's massive knowledge, but their questioning thought began it. Their story-telling broke the ground for science, as well as for literature.

It's no wonder that so many of their stories are of the kind we know as fantasy. They had a huge unknown to explore, and fantasy best explores the unknown. They had to define the intangible without the aid of a jargon, and fantasy substitutes symbols for jargon; it's the algebra of literature. The stories that reached us have lasted because they were memorable, and fantasy, dealing in the extraordinary, is most memorable. A simple verbal form, when it deals with emotion, should step easily into poetry, and fantasy steps easily into poetry. It's not remarkable that, of the folktales we know, so many should be fantasy. What does seem remarkable is that we of today should be divided, some of us uncertain, in our approach to fantasy.

This oldest and freest kind of thinking—which abandons restrictive detail of favour of essentials, or which in its search for a wider view demands the freedom to fly—is an inheritance as old as story itself. Neanderthal Man, explaining the rituals of death, must have done so through fantasy. We should be perfectly at home with it, should know with the experience of millennia what it is doing and how. Yet somewhere, somehow, understanding has broken down.

When you mention fantasy to any large group, there's often an uneasy shuffling. Half of the company, or rather less, sits forward with a happy smile; the rest sit back looking baffled. What has happened?

I first met Hoban's *The Sea-Thing Child* when I happened to be acting as writer-in-residence at a Sydney college. The story captivated me, and I read it to a class of trainee-teachers during a period on children's literature. The whole group received it in puzzled silence. At last they managed an honest comment: yes, it sounded good, but—what was it *about?*

Now these were tertiary students; given any real-life story they might have thought beyond or short of the author's own thinking—that is the license of story. If the story had been complex, or understated, they would have searched for its theme and known how to go about it; no real-life story would have left them completely baffled. And *The Sea-Thing*

Child is not one of those fantasies that invite you to explore a wide, undefined area; it's a story of masterly simplicity, exploring one simple area of human experience.

I was so astonished that I did the wrong thing. Instead of leading them up to the bafflement and letting them find the way through, I simply gasped. "But—hasn't anyone ever been afraid? Of something that should be normal and natural? Hasn't anyone dreaded starting school? Or panicked at the thought of marriage?

That started a quite enthusiastic discussion. They were all right now; someone had told them what the story was about.

To me this is saddening. To like or dislike so ancient a system of thought is one thing; to be baffled by it is another. But one can't help noticing that, to many keen readers, fantasy is a doubtful sort of lightweight nonsense fit only for tinies. They would like to reject it outright, but this is a problem because every now and then someone produces another fantasy that can't be rejected or labelled as lightweight nonsense. And so, with puzzled resignation, they can only regret that some substantial authors should over-indulge their imagination in this way, or perhaps retreat from reality.

This is a lack of comprehension, for substantial authors don't generally aim to produce either fantasy or realism; they aim to produce a story, exploring a certain concept. They will produce it in whatever form the story seems to demand. They will go on using fantasy because story, that powerful system of thought, will go on demanding it. Luckily.

Even the makers of visual story, on stage or film, can't resist fantasy. This is less fortunate; for fantasy, which most extends the power and freedom of the mind, most often also *depends* on that power and freedom. Even the sort of trick photography that merely shrinks or enlarges characters can't do it with the rightness and realness of a mental picture; and puppets or animations can be quite destructive. Fantasy is a natural region only of the mind. Yet one can't blame any maker of story for extending creativity into fantasy. One can only ask what has happened at the receiving end.

Perhaps the attempts to make fantasy visual must share in the blame. And perhaps that stern old nineteenth-century materialism has confused us all, writers and readers too. For one has to admit that there has been some basis for an uneasy approach to fantasy, and some writers have seemed as uncertain as some readers. A lot has been written that is truly lightweight and nonsensical; fantasy has sometimes been truly a self-indulgence.

Surely anyone with experience as a children's editor must know how often children are an excuse for the sort of whimsical non-story that I used to call "personal daydream," inflicted on this captive audience in the name of fantasy. But fantasy is story; it shares the object of story. It may be solemn or poetic or the purest fun, but it is always concerned with life. It may speak in symbols, or abandon the restrictions of life, but it should always explore and illuminate life.

In my childhood, when fantasy was suspect but-of-course-there-was-Lewis-Carroll, confused writers used to avoid the problem of unreality by writing stories that ended, "and then she woke up. It was only a dream." I remember how letdown I used to feel, having the rug pulled out from under me like that. But *Alice in Wonderland* is not a fantasy; it's the very successful, lifelike story of a dream. In fantasy the dream is always real.

I don't know which came first, the hen or the egg—whether pseudo-fantasy, from writers without purpose, caused the dichotomy among readers, or whether a helplessly uncritical approach by readers encouraged the pseudo-fantasy; but I should think it very likely, by now, that each of these factors works on and helps to perpetuate the other. Librarians will know, as I do not, who first uttered the famous apology that one still hears quoted: "Fantasy begins by asking you to suspend disbelief." No greater disservice could have been done to fantasy than to offer for it this apology and excuse. A thousand maiden ladies, on first-name terms with raindrops and roses, must have rubbed their hands and reached for their pens.

Fantasy is story, and no story has any business to begin by asking you weakly to suspend disbelief. It is the business of story to require and work for your belief. It may be more difficult in fantasy, but that is the writer's affair; no one is forcing him to try. If he invites you to go flying with him, the very least he can do is to build a strong pair of wings. The freedom of fantasy is not license: if it abandons the laws and logic of reality, it must provide other laws and logic to govern itself. It may invent circumstances to suit its purpose, but the purpose must be story's obligation to explore life and humanity. It has great strengths: the power of the extraordinary, the broad definition of symbol, the evocative voice of poetry; having them, it mustn't also ask for your weak and complaisant credulity. If fantasy is not strong, it is nothing.

If you begin, as a special concession to fantasy, by abandoning disbelief, you begin by abandoning your critical judgement on all these functions. You wouldn't dream of approaching a real-life story in such a way. So it's hardly a wonder if the approach to fantasy is often uncertain, if writers as well as readers lose their conviction and purpose.

It would be a strange defeat for our knowledgeable age: the loss of a mental skill that was used confidently by men and women wearing string or skins or homespun. People who stood on the verge of a world seen but not yet known used it to explore their visions of the stars and the wind. Having no safeguards against material want, yet they had room in their thinking to explore intangibles: the fear and fascination of the sea, the silent mystery of snow, the terrible stroke of lightning, the menace of the dark, the lurking unknown of the forest. They explored emotion: fear and jealousy, loss and endurance, loneliness and companionship. And their thinking is still relevant, still human and moving.

There's the Australian story of Balyet, the lovely young girl who faded into an echo: not for love, as the Greek Echo did but few living people have done, but for loneliness, frustration, and despair as many people have done.

And how can you read without compassion those universal tales of the vanishing fairy-wife?—beautiful, tender, romantic—and vanishing, because the human husband could not fulfil her terms. It's a theme that will be relevant as long as men and women fall in love with their dreams and ache to find reality only human; the theme of a million stories and poems to come. And none of them will handle it with a deeper or more poetic insight than the tales of the fairy-wife who is always lost.

The pervasive theme of man-into-beast, as we know it best, has been taken over by the nursery; frog princes, cat princesses, caged-bird heroines, Beauty and the Beast, have all their happy endings. But I have met the theme in a folklore that never reached the nursery, and I can't believe in the happy ending. The theme is too painful; for me it threw a whole book into shadow. Nor could I feel it as some old nightmare, irrelevant to life. In those days too there must have been deforming accidents and diseases, insanity with flashes of insight, a moment's breaking of tabu. Men could suddenly become beasts then as now, when they may wake from a blind red mist, or a drink too many, to find themselves monsters; when a trained, athletic body can become in one moment a quadriplegic hulk.

And we whose vision is so much broader, who have turned magic into mathematics and walked on the magic moon—we who have advanced so far that some of us have lost touch with fantasy—do we use it only from habit and tradition, or by caprice? Not always, at any rate. There's the Earthsea trilogy, exploring the darkness of self: in what different form could that have been better done?

There's science fiction, pouring out under the pressure of demand: you'd almost think that we too, like the people from the age of folklore, stood on the verge of a world seen but not yet known. There was the sweeping success of The Lord of the Rings: it almost seems as if we too had felt a darkness of Mordor. Supermen, bionic men, Dr Who: you could almost believe that we too needed heroes.

The Borrowers, Mistress Mascham's Repose, The Lost Farm, The Mouse and His Child: you'd almost think that we, in our turn, explored the condition of being very small in a world of superpowers. Talking animals still, and in spite of wiser counsels: you might think we suspected that man's dominion ought to be more brotherly.

No, I don't think we're in danger of losing fantasy; not as long as we go on needing it. In fact, I might suggest to a superpower or two that whenever they notice a regrettable upsurge of fantasy they should take heed: the people are exploring values and imponderables. They're trying on new visions, debating questions, working it out in algebra.

And to those who believe that realty is solidest and soundest I might say, in my Australian way, fair enough; but how do you decide, in this century, what is real and what is fantasy? Since Einstein has shown that truth is what you see from a certain point of view, since physics has proved by its own laws that it can't exist, since it's now all right to wear a copper band for rheumatism and almost all right to spank your child if he's naughty, since the planet Venus is an intruder into our universe, since as many minor mysteries as ever remain unexplained, who will have the temerity to say, "This is real," without adding cautiously, "as far as we know?" In the 1940s we plumbed the horrors of fantasy and they were real. Is there no room in reality for wonder too?

There's a new story hovering at the edge of my mind—or it may be a story, that will have to be proved. I would have been working at it, weighing and handling the stone, if I hadn't been trying to work out what writers do and why. But if this wild idea does prove to be a story, it will be a fantasy in which two children wander for a long time in my country and discover magical things. They'll find a mountain being burnt away underneath by fire; a sleeping pool whose waters rise and fall as it breathes; a beach where they can gather gems instead of shells; a lake that vanishes and is restored; another whose waters wander round its bed, now here, now there. They will meet, in darkness, their ancient ancestor made of opal; camp by a salt-water river where, at evening, fresh water rises through the rocks for thirsty travellers; tumble through a swamp into mysterious gardens deep under crystal water. The story will be fantasy, yet all these magical things will in fact be real; places and things that do exist, or did until lately. So perhaps it's only because I'm Australian that I think there should be room in reality for wonder.

For fantasy is only a way of looking at things: looking at them with wonder. And surely wonder is a real and hopeful experience. We who share in story the visions and values, the humour and sadness, the poetry and the whole homely business of living, surely we would choose to share wonder too.

Aidan Chambers

All of a Tremble to See His Danger

Aidan Chambers

is a critic, author and lecturer. He has written the text *Introducing Books to Children* (Heinemann, 1973) and a collection of essays, *Booktalk; Occasional Writing on Literature and Children* (U.S. edition: Harper & Row, 1985). His novels include *Breaktime* (U.S. edition: Harper & Row, 1979); *Seal Secret* (U.S. edition: Harper & Row, 1981); *Dance on My Grave* (U.S. edition: Harper & Row, 1983); and *The Present Takers* (U.S. edition: Harper & Row, 1984). He is the co-founder of *Signal: Approaches to Children's Books* with his wife Nancy, with whom he shared the 1982 Eleanor Farjeon Award for distinguished services to children's books. Chambers was also honored for excellence in literary criticism in 1978 by the Children's Literature Association.

If I'd a knowed what a trouble it was to make a book
I wouldn't a tackled it.—Huck Finn

IT IS A RARE PRIVILEGE to be invited to deliver this annual lecture in honor of that gifted teacher and advocate of children's literature, May Hill Arbuthnot. I am conscious of the compliment, and thank you for it. No less am I grateful to all of you here in Little Rock for adding the further compliment of bringing me to your city to speak at this impressive occasion.

When I heard the news that I was to come to Arkansas, I immediately thought of the book that has been a favorite of mine from my youth, and which has considerably influenced my work as an author. The long eastern border of your state is described by the Mississippi. It is, of course, on that amazing river and on its Arkansas banks that so many of *The Adventures of Huckleberry Finn* take place. I celebrated the news that I was actually to see the setting of Mark Twain's novel by giving myself the pleasure of reading it again.

I know *Huckleberry Finn* reached its centenary last year; I expect you heard quite enough about it then to last you for a while. But I want to tell you how I was again struck by its modernity. I find it hard to believe that *Huckleberry Finn* first appeared over a hundred years ago. Many books written since then—*Catcher in the Rye,* for example, which owes its inspiration to *Huck*—seem so much more dated, not half so alive and fresh. And again, I realized just how much the book has taught me, and goes on teaching me. About adolescence and the things that matter most at that time of life; about how to tell stories; about how to read and how not to; and about the function of adolescent literature as a metaphor, a way by which we examine the social, moral, political, and other deepest questions of our time.

You see, for me, what you call young adult literature and we in Britain often call teenage literature is not simply *for* adolescents. It is written on behalf of them too. By which I mean it represents the adolescent view of life not only to young people but to adults as well. Young adult literature is not, to my mind, a ghetto intended for and restricted to those who live in that patch. Nor is it a genre, for it includes work in many genres, such as detective stories and science fiction, romances whether of the sentimental or the fantastic kind, naturalistic novels about contemporary life, and so on. No, the features that set it apart are that its central concern is the adolescent experience, and that its depiction of adolescence becomes an image for, a metaphor of, the whole of life. The result should be a book in which both adolescent and adult readers mutually find significant meaning for their own, individual lives.

Presented April 25, 1986, at the Fine Arts Auditorium, University of Arkansas, Little Rock. The 1986 Arbuthnot Lecture is sponsored by Scott, Foresman and Company in cooperation with the Association for Library Service to Children.

It is about these topics I'd like to speak rather than about *Huckleberry Finn.* But I'd like to view them through the eyes of that proto-adolescent Huck Finn himself, and so I have headed each chapter of this short story about today's young adult literature with some of Huck's words, sayings of such pith and moment that they reach across the intervening century without any loss of pertinence.

**It was like being born again,
I was so glad to find out who I was**

It is a truism to say that adolescence is a time when we seek for an identity, and that the literature written for and on behalf of adolescents explores that experience as much as or more than any other. Huck is right: when you find out who you are, it is like being born again. And the phrase he uses tells us something present-day literature for the young often omits, or at any rate neglects. The experience of finding out who you are is not simply to do with the emotions or with the intellect or with the social and political constraints and frustrations of the society you happen to live in. Rather, it is spiritual in nature, encompassing all those other aspects of life and transcending them.

One of the problems for a writer on behalf of young adults these days is to know how to deal with spiritual experience. Years ago, when people conventionally believed in a God they could agree about, acceptable patterns for stories about spiritual experience were easy to come by. Now, when there is dispute about whether there are any gods at all, never mind agreement about one, the patterns are threadbare and faded. Finding a way of making a convincing narrative about spiritual truths is therefore one of the challenges that face us. Some of our best writers for the young are finding metaphors that work. Virginia Hamilton is one; Patricia Wrightson, your 1985 lecturer from Australia, is another; Alan Garner is achieving it in my country. I have not exhausted the list.

When I look at *Huckleberry Finn* to find out how Twain did it I am astonished and delighted again by the relevance of his methods to our needs today. Twain lived at a time when the agreed spiritual formulas were still usable. He not only rejects them and does something else, he turns his solution into a critique of the conventional modes. So the first thing he teaches any writer about the craft of writing for young people is this: Look at what is currently being written and accepted as respectable, and turn it on its head. That way you'll strike closer to the truth.

How did Twain do it? First, he has Huck adopted by the Widow Douglas, whose benevolent desire to improve him finds expression in the conventional religious instruction of the day. She promises Huck his dearest desires now and a heavenly life after death if he learns to pray, reads his Bible, and does as he's told. He tries it and it doesn't seem to work, but he's a long-suffering boy and tolerant so he assumes it is his own fault not the Widow's. Then Miss Watson is introduced into the household. She is a woman of unhuggable nature whose main concern is to improve Huck's social manners by threatening him with hell. Huck finds this less than appealing but he puts up with it by salving himself with his wit. It is, however, the violent affection of his natural father that finally drives him from the Widow's shelter and onto the river and into the company of Miss Watson's fugitive slave, Jim.

In other words, Twain begins with everyday life as most young people knew it and by force of circumstances over which his proto-adolescent has no control brings Huck into a situation that faces him with the central questions of his own personality and of the society of his day. Huck is trying to escape from adult requirements, whether they be well-intentioned or ill, and to opt for the irresponsibility of boyhood. But in making his escape he is thrown into company with another escapee, a man oppressed by one of the most troublesome social and political, not to say moral, problems of the time.

After that, the story of Huck's adolescence is inextricably mixed up with the story of Jim. This is plot making of the most elegant kind in which all the threads of the narrative, whether of action, character, theme or setting, are integrated into a coherent, resonant whole. For the adolescent truth that Twain is giving shape to is this: In order to know who you are you have to be free to become who you wish to be. The central concern of adolescence, therefore, is freedom to be.

Robert Cormier's *The Chocolate War* is a good example of the same technique at work. He sets his story in a Roman Catholic boys' school run by monks, where you would expect the spiritual values of life to be high on the agenda, gives bullies the run of the place, and inspires one boy to stand against the mob. This is *Tom Brown's Schooldays* stood on its head; it is the Christ story reworked in a twentieth-century school where Christ is supposed to be the ideal and guide; it is a metaphor of the greatest political evil of our day—the evil of state-organized crime against individuals who in the end have no power against it but the strength of their spirit, which means the strength that comes from confidence in your own death. Yet *The Chocolate War* is entirely about adolescence; Cormier's book succeeds because it speaks convincingly and significantly on behalf of the state of being Jerry explores for us.

Jerry learns that you get to know who you want to be by obtaining the freedom to be. Huck learns that too. When he says finding out who he was was like being born again his words are laden, as they often are, with a complicated irony. At the time, near the end of the book, he is searching for Jim who is locked up on the Phelps' farm. Huck arrives, is greeted, he knows not why, like a long-lost brother. He plays for time, hoping to find out who the Phelps think he is. At last the Phelps let the name slip. They think he is Tom Sawyer. And to Huck, knowing this is such a relief it is like being born again.

Here we have another instance of what has happened throughout the book: Huck's identity is imposed on him by the adults on whom he depends. To the Widow Douglas, for instance, he is a dutiful adopted son; to the Grangerfords he is a recently orphaned offspring of a respectable Arkansas farmer; on one occasion he even pretends he is a girl. All this role play, this trying-on of parts, is literally turned into a theatrical image during one of the longest sequences in the book when Huck becomes stagehand, bit-part player, and apprentice to the King and the Duke in their fraudulent theatre, the sole purpose of which is to defraud innocent people of their material possessions. A century ago your material possessions were often called your substance, a word that in our day and in Twain's might also mean the essence of your being. One could hardly hope for a more tightly constructed metaphor.

Every adolescent has to deal with the realization that, so far, his or her identity has been imposed by adults. Breaking free from these impositions is one of the struggles of that time of life. In order to achieve freedom they begin by trying to shrug off the identities given them as children. They go on to attack the orthodox social and psychological categories society at large presents them with as teenagers, seeing in them simply another imposition. Instead, they demand an authority based on their individual uniqueness, and on their own revision of established customs and laws. In other words they become uncomfortable spiritual visionaries holding out ideals of freedom and behaviour we should all live by. And because of the way they assert themselves they often sound like political revolutionaries, which is why adults feel there is something subversive about even the best behaved adolescents.

The comic side of this manifestation is that it is all talk. At no time are we more loquacious than during adolescence. Never are our thoughts more vaultingly ambitious. Never are we so capable of unsparing honesty. And yet never are our lives so little conducted through action. All adolescents pretend to adults and even to each other that just the opposite is the case. And they constantly hunt for significant action in which to involve themselves, the kind of action that will give honorable expression to their visionary ambitions.

That story has been written many times. *Catcher in the Rye* is one version. Robert Cormier's *After the First Death* is another. Much of the work of Paul Zindel—and there's an author who owes a debt to Twain if anyone does—is about teenagers hunting for significant actions by which to define their personalities. Louise Fitzhugh treats it in *Nobody's Family Is Going to Change,* and it is at the core of Mildred D. Taylor's sequence of novels beginning with *Roll of Thunder, Hear My Cry.*

In her outstanding book, *The Adolescent Idea: Myths of Youth and the Adult Imagination,* Patricia Meyer Spacks, the feminist critic from Yale, traces this very line in the literature written since the eighteenth century on behalf of adults. She demonstrates how adolescents as individuals "suffer uncertainty, absence of power." Characters like Salinger's Holden Caulfield and Doris Lessing's Martha Quest "epitomize two typical adolescent manifestations: the need of the young person to invent himself or herself, and the problematic relation of reality and fantasy in youthful experience."[1]

Perhaps I find myself quoting that particular sentence from Spacks because it appeals to my own experience as a person and goes to the heart of my work as an author. My two novels *Breaktime* and *Dance on My Grave* try to explore just what that generalization "the need of the young person to *invent* himself or herself" actually means. How do we invent ourselves and what does it feel like? We all know there are conflicts between our fantasies about ourselves and the reality that confronts us. But how do we come to terms with them? As I wrote, my protagonists showed me just how true it is, as Spacks says, that adolescence is "a crucial period of ambiguous potential,"[2] that we live then in a constant condition of desire, the kind of desire that "supplies energy, generates conflict, makes action—the stuff of novels. It also raises questions of value."[3] The deeper I dug beneath the surface of the narrative of each book, the more I kept stubbing my intellectual toes on the fact that once you are grappling with questions of human value you are dealing with matters of the spirit. So my own novels, never mind other people's, have forced me to a reconsideration of the spiritual aspect of adolescent experience and the narrative problems raised by telling a story about it, given the nature of the society we live in. As I haven't yet finished writing the resulting novel, I can't say more just now. But a few words from Huck Finn point us in the right direction.

All right, then, I'll go to hell

I talked a moment ago about how the search for an identity is a central concern of teenage, and so it is. But one of the many interesting things about Huck Finn is that he doesn't seem to suffer much in the way of an identity crisis. I mean, he doesn't moon around for hours on end wondering who on earth he is. Perhaps the reason is that most adolescents don't suffer identity crises. After all, in order to have an identity crisis I suppose you must already have an identity to have a crisis about. Surely, it is middle-aged people who have identity crises, not adolescents. And like many people in a crisis they tend to project their problems onto others whom they envy or dislike, feel threatened by or want help from, or of course love enough to feel secure with.

Which explains a lot about adolescents who appear in fiction written on behalf of adults. Spacks shows how adolescent characters are there used to make statements about adult, and mostly middle-aged concerns. Spacks finishes her book with these words:

> The young embody our most profound vulnerabilities and our most intimate strengths. They speak to us of our past and of our future. We can imagine them as licensed transgressors, surrogates for ourselves, or as prophets of salvation. . . . The mythology of adolescence, recorded in fiction . . . tells us of ourselves, our ancestors, and our descendants.[4]

In literature for our adult selves we exploit adolescence as a critical viewpoint from which to look at ourselves and reassess what we are and still might be. In some fiction adolescence is merely used to confirm an adult's prejudices about the world, as I think is the case in Anthony Burgess' novel *The Clockwork Orange,* which seems to me to describe much more the hell-on-earth created by middle-aged men than a world desired by teenagers. Its clash of fantasy and reality tells us more about Burgess and his contemporaries than about adolescence, and is a good example of how adult authors employ adolescent characters to arouse and shift their own generation's guilt.

Throughout Spacks' book, though she deals with this subject in literature from the eighteenth century to the present, there is not one mention of *Huckleberry Finn.* Understandable, because it is considered a novel *for* young readers and is therefore excluded from her range. But also, perhaps, it is ignored because it requires a definition of the difference between the adult exploitation of youth in literature and literature written on behalf of adolescence. And this isn't a definition literary critics are prepared to make. They prefer to think that there is no difference, that the books published for young readers are simply diminished versions of fiction written for adults. Even a critic of such notable sensibility as T. S. Eliot can only allow himself to call *Huckleberry Finn* a masterpiece, which he does in his Introduction to the Cresset edition, by telling us at the same time that it "does not fall into the category of juvenile fiction."[5] One suspects Eliot thought that a book couldn't be both a masterpiece of world literature *and* a fiction written for young readers. I hesitate to suggest such a view for a critic of his standing, but I wonder if he could only think like that (and he is far from alone, his in fact being the commonplace view) because he had not understood the concept of writing on behalf of a state of life that still lives inside you, even though you are past the age when it is the socially evident and psychologically pertinent expression of your existence.

In other words, I am saying that though I am fifty-one, and presently enjoying the pleasures and pains associated with middle age, there is still alive inside me the state of being I experienced as a sixteen-year-old adolescent. I do not simply mean I remember that time, and look back at it with whatever degree of nostalgia or distaste my present personality dictates. Rather I mean that adolescence still informs me, is still active in me. Just as my childhood is. And I am glad. Indeed, one of the values that distinguishes the best of literature written on behalf of childhood and youth is that it helps maintain and refresh those states within us. That is part of its purpose as a literary form, one of the reasons why we need it and should attend to it whether or not we are professionally involved. Childhood and adolescence are not, after all, the sole possessions of children and teenagers. They belong to us all.

I think Mark Twain discovered this through his own writing. *The Adventures of Tom Sawyer* is a book about boyhood written by an adult looking back at his experience of it. Twain knew this, which is why he told William Howells: "It is *not* a boy's book, at all. It will only be read by adults. It is only written for adults."[6] He was wrong about boys not reading it because he wasn't allowing for the fact that children are quite as capable of entering into the adult view of themselves as adults are of reentering childhood, if the fiction enables them to do so. *Tom Sawyer* does. But he was right about it being a book written on behalf of adults. The narrator's tone of voice puts years between the storyteller and his protagonist.

My author's instinct—I have no other evidence to go on—tells me he almost at once felt uneasy about what he had done. In a sense, and to couch what I'm trying to say in crude shorthand, he had betrayed his boyhood, warped what it had been and had meant, by making use of it, perhaps for nostalgic, perhaps for commercial reasons. At any rate, I fancy the emotional pressure was strong in him to make amends. Besides, he was not an entirely happy man around the time *Tom Sawyer* was written. This small-town boy from the frontier life of Missouri had settled for the old world habits of the cultural establishment of New England and had thus cut himself off from his roots. He was playing a part he was neither born to nor personally suited for. There's cause for a middle-aged identity crisis if ever I saw one!

It was the honesty of the man that provoked him to write *Huckleberry Finn.* He could have put *Tom Sawyer* behind him, suppressed the sense of guilt about his betrayal of his youth. Plenty of writers work that trick and survive happily enough. But no author can. As I try to explain in my recently published volume *Booktalk,* writers make books of whatever kind their readers want. If they want nostalgic tales of childhood, a writer can supply them. But authors can't do that. They work according to the truth of their experience, and if they deliberately warp that truth they lose the self-respect of their vocation.

Twain interests me because he was at first a writer, bashing out copy for newspapers and the popular press. But he discovered himself as an author and then wanted to reveal the truth he knew in the form of the best fictional codes he could conceive. By the time he wrote *Tom Sawyer* this was the crisis of his life, the moment when he finally chose his identity. He is one of those people whose adolescence extends long into adulthood, because it is not till then that they meet the experience that shifts their state of being. The result in Twain is that he authored *Huckleberry Finn,* from which, according to Ernest Hemingway, comes all modern American literature, which Willa Cather lists as one of the three American books she feels have the possibility of a long, long life (the others are *The Scarlet Letter* and *The Country of the Pointed Firs*), which T. S. Eliot among others calls a masterpiece, which numerous authors have acknowledged owing a debt, including that giant of twentieth-century literature, James Joyce, and which uncounted critics have heaped praise upon.

Twain's adolescent crisis, suffered in middle age, gave us this wonder, the first great book written on behalf of youth, the prototype for young adult literature, a sampler of craft skill, a progenitor of scores of books since. Lionel Trilling, in what is to my mind one of the best essays about *Huckleberry Finn*, says that its greatness lies "primarily in its power of telling the truth." He is also one of the few critics who acknowledges that an essential part of its greatness is "that it succeeds first as a boys' book.[7] It tells the truth about being an adolescent—not the adult-reflecting truth, but the truth as an adolescent sees it. *Huckleberry Finn*'s essence lies in the fact that it is a novel, the first to achieve it, in which the author stays true to the adolescent self he once openly was and still secretly is. But it does even more than that. While honoring his youth, the author takes with him into his novel the knowledge of life he has acquired since, and transposes it by his craft skill into knowledge that a teenager can convincingly discover.

In Twain's case, this was done by investing the whole of his self in Huck. The unhappy man suffering a middle-aged identity crisis is really describing himself when Huck says, on the first page of the book: "I couldn't stand it no longer, I lit out. I got into my old rags . . . and was free and satisfied.''[8] Only a sentence later Tom Sawyer drags him back with promises of a different kind of satisfaction. But by chapter 3 he knows it won't do: ''all that stuff was just . . . Tom Sawyer's lies,'' Huck sneers, and runs for freedom.

This is, I repeat, crude shorthand. Authors of fiction are always both more and less than their characters. That's why Scott Fitzgerald is right when he says somewhere in his *Notebooks:* ''There never was a good biography of a good novelist. There couldn't be. He is too many people.'' And anyhow, what has it to do with Huck's decision to go to hell?

The moment when he makes this alarming choice occurs near the end of the book. In order to understand its significance and why the religious imagery has an ironic reach that exceeds its colloquial grasp, we must recall what is happening at the time. Huck is agonizing about his friendship with Jim and has just written a letter to Miss Watson, telling her where she can find her slave. He does this because he can think of no other way to save Jim from soon being sold to strangers. He has even tried kneeling down and promising to give up sin if God will lend a hand. But that doesn't work; he can't even say the words. He knows why. ''My heart warn't right. . . . I warn't square. . . . I was playing double.'' Betrayal is the problem again. The letter to Miss Watson is a desperate attempt to set himself square by doing his duty. But that doesn't work either. He recalls all he and Jim have done together, and knows that to give him away to Miss Watson or to anybody else would be the greatest betrayal of all: the betrayal of common humanity, never mind what the artificial, customary laws of society may demand. He looks at the letter and realizes that for the first time in his life, ''I'd got to decide, for ever, betwixt two things.''

I mentioned earlier the desire adolescents feel for involvement in significant action. Huck now finds out what it means when that desire becomes a reality. It is the moment when a young person realizes that the power s/he needs to bring thoughtful vision into touch with active reality lies at last in her/his grasp. This is the real crisis of adolescence, a crisis of choice between possibilities of what you might be, and finding at the same moment that each possibility bears the potential of a terrible cost. Huck's dilemma dramatizes the choice at its most stark. If he chooses to give Jim away, his reward will be a kind of comfort, but the finally cruel and self-despising comfort of weakness, for thereafter he will be a creature who must settle for the world as he finds it. Choose to grasp the vision, as he puts it, of ''stealing Jim from slavery'' and the reality of action could be the discomforture of a kind of hell. In Huck's case, it would be the hell of imprisonment by men here on earth and the prophecy of those same men that he will suffer the Devil's hell in the hereafter.

In Huck, the crisis of all adolescents who seek their freedom to be, and the crisis of freedom in the society of his day meet in the decision he must make about his relationship with Jim. No earthly law or custom is much use at that moment. Everything depends on your view of your own death, what it means to you and what it portends. That's why Huck's words are so precise and why in the end this insignificant boy's journey down the mighty Mississippi with an insignificant slave is a spiritual odyssey of universal proportions. And as we watch him make his choice, we are, in his own words, "all of a tremble to see his danger."

The narrative and ironic elegance here is astonishing. Twain builds his story so that from start to finish every episode is a meditation on freedom. Which can be put another way, not in Huck's words this time but in someone else's:

You wouldn't a ben here, 'f it hadn't a ben for Jim

Human freedom is always conditional. My freedom depends upon someone else's; so does everyone's. Twain explores some of those conditions.

Jim and Huck personify two extremes. In Jim we see the conditions of other people's freedom at their most cruel. He is not only a slave, he is a fugitive slave, a state of being in which there is even less freedom for himself than he would have as a law-abiding captive. He daren't show his face in public lest he be arrested, he can't live in what passes for his own home, nor be with his family. He is a slave in hiding, ever on the run, subject to the whim of everyone who stumbles across him. Huck, on the other hand, is the nearest anyone can get to being a free-roaming spirit. He can do whatever he likes, restricted only by the limits of his own wit and cunning. He even has money to help him—the money he banked with Judge Thatcher after the adventure with Tom Sawyer told of in the earlier book. But there is one condition that confines him, whether he likes it or not: the birthright of his sonship. He cannot escape his parentage until he comes to terms with it. No one can.

At the start Huck plays at being the son of Widow Douglas. But that's just a game; he knows he can give up the part whenever he wants. Then, however, his real father turns up, claims him back, takes him to his shack and locks him up—a literal image of the emotional and psychological truth of a relationship which cannot simply be walked away from.

Huck escapes from the shack by digging his way out, another action that resonates symbolically. In the very next chapter he falls in with Jim and remains with him for the rest of the book. Why does he do this, when Jim threatens his physical freedom in every way? For the simple reason that Huck invests in Jim the conditions of fatherhood. Thereafter, he serves his apprenticeship as a son to the fugitive. Lionel Trilling is right in suggesting that the boy and the slave "form a family, a primitive community—and it is a community of saints."[9]

Trilling's spiritual language is accurate and appropriate. Jim is more of a father than Huck's natural father ever was, sustaining him, providing for him, saving him from mortal and emotional danger. (Jim it is, you'll remember, who rescues Huck from drowning, and who finds the rotting corpse of Huck's dead father and keeps the boy from the trauma of seeing, or even knowing about it, until the very last page of the book.) In every sense, Jim is in loco parentis to Huck. But it is Huck who maintains this state of affairs by remaining with him, by protecting him, and by aiding Jim's escape, just as a son would, even though he knows that by doing so he puts his own life in jeopardy.

No wonder when Huck is suffering the final crisis of his adolescence and is trying to persuade himself to give Jim up—give him up in the legal, worldly sense and give him up in the spiritual sense of betraying his sonship—he tells us how he:

> got to thinking over our trip down the river; and I see Jim before me, all the time, in the day, and in the night-time, sometimes moonlight, sometimes storms, and we a-floating along, talking, and singing, and laughing. But somehow I couldn't seem to strike no places to harden me against him, but only the other kind . . . how good he always was.

This is not simply a description of their life together on the river; it is a lyric account of the spiritually healed state of Huck's being brought about by his relationship with Jim. In more ways than one is it true that, without Jim, Huck wouldn't have been alive. For Jim brings into focus not one main concern of adolescence but two. The first is a concern with freedom. The second is a concern with parents, and especially the crisis between child and father. Jim embodies both. For Huck to obtain his spiritual freedom and gain the self-respect that will allow him to be the man he wants to be, he not only must help Jim obtain his freedom from slavery but he must also come to terms with his dependence upon, his prejudices about, the legacy of his parent. He must lay to rest the brutality he inherited from his bestial, unregenerated natural father. It is not by accident that Twain gives Hamlet's soliloquy "To be, or not to be" to the Duke to mangle in front of Huck and Jim during rehearsals for the Nonesuch Theatre. Indeed, Huck is, to use another Shakespearean image, like a son of Caliban who rejects his natural father and adopts Prospero to God-father him into a new life he has chosen for himself. No writer has explored this aspect of adolescent experience more subtly, nor more intricately than Mark Twain in *Huckleberry Finn*, and few have done it so memorably. Moreover, he works this magic without spoiling the book with what Huck calls:

All the marks of a Sunday school

The family of literature for young readers has its own parentage to live out. It was born of a humble, well-intentioned mother named Simple Didactics, and sired by a cunning but aggressive father called Cheap Commerce. Many children of the family inherited the worst of the genes from both sides. Even now, they stick close to home and carry on the business of telling readers what to think in off-the-shelf stories more notable for the craft of their marketing than the skill of their crafting.

Huckleberry Finn, however, inherited the best genes from both sides and established a new dynasty in the family. Denying the impulse to tell people *what to think,* Twain designed instead a story that helps people discover *how to think*. Huck is a full-blown character but he is also a representative of his readers. His story is composed of a sequence of images for his readers to think with alongside Huck.

Nowhere, for example, is slavery condemned. Instead the novel presents images of slavery: Jim's racial and social slavery; Huck's slavery to identities imposed on him; other characters' slavery, like Miss

Watson's, to conventional behaviour. The plot is composed of variations on capture and escape. Even the Mississippi is part of this pattern. The river, a road that moves, is Huck and Jim's route to freedom, and yet also holds them captive. Sitting on their floating home, the escapees are safe from their would-be human owners but are captive to the dispassionate river, which takes them where it will, once, at a vital moment, carrying them past the point where, by leaving it, Jim would have gained his release.

The river holds them captive and it also captivates them. Huck is only ever truly himself, the person who will live inside the man he wishes to become, when he is drifting down the river, observing the natural world, talking and laughing with Jim, and thinking his thoughts. It is on one such happy occasion that he says to Jim, "This is nice, I wouldn't want to be no-where else but here," and receives Jim's truth-sharp reply, "Well, you wouldn't a been here, 'f it hadn't a been for Jim."

Rather than tell us, Sunday-school fashion, what all this means, we are left to think it out for ourselves. The images are vividly there: the river that carries to freedom by holding captive; the free-roaming white boy at home on a drifting raft with his surrogate father, the black slave Jim; Huck's pleasure in his well-being; that one line of dialogue to make active the potentials of meaning. And not merely one meaning, but many, some of them ironically paradoxical.

Twain works like this all the way through the book, which is why I say that it has so much to tell us about how to read and how not to. When the novel first appeared, its challenge to the reader to enter it and resolve the indeterminate meanings for him/herself led the Sunday-school kind of reader—the one who wants to be told what to think—to attack it for its "very low grade morality," as the Concord, Massachusetts, library committee so famously phrased it, as well as for its "systematic use of bad grammar and an employment of rough, coarse, inelegant expressions."[10] Which brings me, inevitably, to the attacks made on it these days for being racially offensive.

Even as I write this at home in England one of our leading poets, Adrian Mitchell, has sent a letter to one of our leading magazines, *The Listener,* complaining that *Huckleberry Finn* is

> far worse than offensive, it is poisonous.
>
> Imagine what a black child must feel when the book—with its 200 uses of the word [nigger]—is read aloud in class: "Whenever *that word* is read out, the other kids stare at me and some of them grin."
>
> Now *Huckleberry Finn* is a great novel. And Mark Twain was one of the foremost champions of black people in the 19th century. . . . But he couldn't foresee what the word "nigger" would become. . . . If we lived in a society of racial harmony, it would be easy. A little historical explanation of the use of the word would precede a reading to a class and all would be well. But we live in an England where racial attacks are commonplace.
>
> I believe that if Mark Twain were faced with a class of black and white children in England or the States today . . . he would read *Huck Finn,* but he would change the word "nigger" to "black man," "black woman," "black child." . . . I'd like to see a new edition based on such tiny but important substitutions.[11]

The challenge to readers goes on. What the Concord library objection a hundred years ago and Adrian Mitchell's of 1986 make starkly obvious is how discomforting even sophisticated readers find a combination of irony and the demotic—the everyday speech of everyday people.

To start with, Twain certainly knew about the word *nigger.* It was poisonous in his day and was always meant to be. That's why he uses it so often and so pointedly, as in the much-quoted exchange between Huck and Sally Phelps: " '. . . anybody hurt?' 'No 'm. Killed a nigger.' 'Well, it's lucky; because sometimes people do get hurt.' " As Huck says in another context, "Human beings *can* be awful cruel to one another."

Leave aside for now the question of what should be done in classrooms, about which I would have a lot to say given the time. What I must say here is that for a poet who deals in irony to suggest that the irony that helps make *Huck* what it is—an attack on slavery and on racial prejudice—should be softened by the removal of one of the words that point up the irony I find depressing. It is another version of wanting literature to tell us what to think instead of dealing with how it is that people come to think what they do think.

Twain knew what he was doing; but there is one aspect of his treatment of Jim that, in my estimation, partly explains the charges of racism. It is another irony that the cause is a weakness within one of the book's great qualities! I mean its innovation with language.

What we have to bear in mind is that the book's tone is comic. It is comic in the classic sense of being about commonplace people whose story has an optimistic, if you like, "happy" ending. It is comic in the sense that it incorporates various kinds of wit and humour, from profound ironies to broad jokes. And it is comic in the sense that it parodies, satirizes, and makes fun of every character and every social group who enter its pages. Jim does not escape this treatment, though it has to be conceded that he is more gently handled than any of the others, including Huck.

Linguistically, most of this comedy takes its cue from the everyday speech of its characters. Ernest Hemingway could say that "All modern American literature comes from one book by Mark Twain called *Huckleberry Finn*"[12] and not be contradicted because it was the first American novel to raise common people's speech to the level of literature, and not only showed the vibrant resources of their language but paid it the respect of serious attention. In my view, one of the reasons for the earliest attacks was that it succeeded. It is ironically satisfying that the first broadside was fired from the heartland of the New England literary establishment, whose writers like Hawthorne, Thoreau, and Ralph Waldo Emerson set the standards of fine literature. These writers took their cue from old England and Europe, where the literary view held that the speech of common people was vulgar, and that the Latin- and Greek-based manners of the rich and educated were the proper styles for novels and poetry.

Twain had accepted this hegemony. *Tom Sawyer* is written according to those rules of the game. Here is a sample:

Saturday morning was come, and all the summer world was bright and fresh, and brimming with life. There was a song in every heart; and if the heart was young the music issued at the lips. There was a cheer in every face, and a spring in every step. The locust trees were in bloom, and the fragrance of the blossoms filled the air. . . .

Tom appeared on the side-walk with a bucket of whitewash and a long-handled brush. He surveyed the fence, and the gladness went out of nature, and a deep melancholy settled down upon his spirit."[13]

The opening of chapter 2. No wonder the old guard loved it. There is murder and theft, low life and irreverence in *Tom Sawyer*, all offenses complained of in *Huckleberry Finn*, but no one was upset by them because they were viewed through the distancing lens of drawing-room discourse. Correct, Latinate grammar, the soothing cadences of familiar phrases ("there was cheer in every face . . . the gladness went out of nature"), and the relaxing knowledge that in the end the narrator will tell us, in suitably amusing fashion, exactly what to think, which he does: "If [Tom] had been a great and wise philosopher, like the writer of this book, he would now have comprehended that work consists of whatever a body is obliged to do, and that play consists of whatever a body is not obliged to do."[14]

This was the stuff Mark Twain reacted against in *Huckleberry Finn*. In recovering his youth, in writing on behalf of his adolescent self, he was, of course, forced to recover the language of his youth, the language of the people around him then, the frontier people of all classes, whom he put into this story about slavery. For the worst slavery of all is slavery to a language that is not your own. In the language of story we define what we are and invent the identity we want for ourselves. Slaves like Jim know that better than anyone. That is why they went on making stories, singing songs, and forming a version of English that was their own.

And here is the weakness. Throughout the book Twain tries to use the grammar, the syntax, the images, the diction of the people on whom his characters are based. He warns us of this in the notice he appends to the front of the book, explaining that he has used a number of what he calls dialects. He was afraid that his readers, and especially those neighbors of his, the New England literary establishment, would not understand, but rather think "that all these characters were trying to talk alike and not succeeding." In other words, he was afraid that his readers wouldn't be able to rise to the challenge of knowing how to read a narrative so unfamiliar in its mix of linguistic styles. He was right to worry; readers down the years have proved that time and again.

But Twain did not restrict himself to demotic grammar, diction, and semantics. He also used phonetically based orthography. And this is the cause of the trouble. If we look at the characters whose speech is rendered phonetically, we see that Judge Thatcher, for example, is treated to none of it; nor is Colonel Sherburn, the man who harangues the lynch mob for their cowardice. No one, in fact, in the upper stratum of society is given anything but conventional grammar and orthography. Tom Sawyer, apart from *ain't*, belongs to this group. Huck's speech is unconventionally spelt more often but not to any great or offputting extent.

The speech of the Phelps, whatever might be said of their grammar, is conventionally spelt, but not their local friends and neighbors, the farmers and their wives who come to dinner. Which perhaps strikes one as strange, given that they belong to the same locality and are social equals. The fact is, Twain sets up the Phelps' neighbors as figures of fun taking part in the farce of Tom Sawyer's rescue of Jim.

Sorted out like this it seems that the lower down the social scale Twain goes and the more he wants to use a character for comic purposes the more he uses phonetically based spelling to represent their speech. Unfortunately, Jim is at the furthest extreme of this technique. In his attempt to bring Jim's speech into the book with as much accuracy and respect as he could, to capture its sounds as well as its style, Twain confused two aims: his aim to investigate his subject matter and his characters through comedy; and his aim to honor the everyday talk of ordinary folk and make it into literature.

The result is that some readers, whether they know why or not, feel Twain is poking malicious fun, is condescending to the socially and educationally least well off, and to Jim in particular. So the white establishment disliked him for the innovation of making common speech equal with their own; and the defenders of Jim disliked him—and still do—for seeming to suggest that black English is a comically uneducated form of establishment white English. That he achieved the first is admirable; that phonetically based spelling as a technique for writing speech is a failure is a lesson we can learn from him. Some writers still haven't learned it; one who has is Virginia Hamilton. Here she is, doing what Twain was aiming to do, in her retelling of black slave stories recently published under the splendid title, *The People Could Fly*. These are the first lines of the first story. I hope you hear when I read them that the essence of their special sound survives even when spoken by a white foreigner who has no live experience of how they sound when they are at home. Please note too that Hamilton uses no strange orthography, except for the dropped *g* in the participle. The story is called "He Lion, Bruh Bear, and Bruh Rabbit."

> Say that he Lion would get up each and every mornin. Stretch and walk around. He'd roar, "ME AND MYSELF. ME AND MYSELF," like that. Scare all the little animals so they were afraid to come outside in the sunshine. Afraid to go huntin or fishin or whatever the little animals wanted to do.
>
> "What we gone do about it?" they asked one another. Squirrel leapin from branch to branch, just scared. Possum playin dead, couldn't hardly move him.
>
> He Lion just went on, stickin out his chest and roarin, "ME AND MYSELF. ME AND MYSELF."[15]

In my country, similar sensitive work has been done by writers like Alan Garner, William Mayne, Jane Gardam, John Gordon, and Jan Mark, who have all brought demotic forms of English into children's and young adult literature, where in the past such accents and dialects were regarded by the literary establishment as illiterate, comic versions of their own use of the language. Twain led the way in this movement and should be applauded for it.

More than this, or rather as part of it, he led the way, and still does, in shifting our understanding about the kind of story that can be written for adolescents. What Huck dismisses as bearing all the marks of a Sunday school is a story he has been told by Tom Sawyer. The kind of story Huck Finn likes is quite different. By entwining the two kinds together in one book Twain creates something new, something of which, to use Huck's words again, it might be said:

It was a grand adventure and mysterious, so it hit him where he lived

Huckleberry Finn begins with an intertextual reference. We're told of its connection with *The Adventures of Tom Sawyer.* And in the first four chapters Tom Sawyer tries to arrange another, similar escapade for his gang. "What's the line of business?" Ben Rogers asks. "Nothing," Tom replies, "only robbery and murder."

Huck refers to Tom's book. Tom refers all his adventures to other people's books. When his gang suggest ways of doing things that Tom dislikes he says they can't "because it ain't in the books . . . Don't you reckon that the people that made the books knows what's the correct thing to do?" I am always amused when I remember that at the same time *Huckleberry Finn* was being finished Robert Louis Stevenson was publishing *Treasure Island*, a story in just the right line of business for Tom. But not for Huck. Tom's reality is based on his fantasies about characters he will never meet, who do things he will never do, and live according to a crudely simple code of good and bad. This is the stuff Huck dismisses as Tom Sawyer's lies that bear all the marks of a Sunday school. So he leaves Tom and follows his own line of business. Huck's reality is based on the everyday events that happen to him; indeed, so firmly is his story fixed in life as it was in those days that the novel is by many counted a valuable historical document. It tells the truth about life yet manages also to be a grand adventure.

At the end of his own two hundred pages, Huck suffers the climax of his adolescence, the crisis of his relationship with Jim, and makes his choice. At that moment the story of his adolescence ends and the story of his adulthood begins. At which point Tom Sawyer appears again, and there follows the long final episode when Tom plays out one of his fantasy adventures, only this time the object of his pretense is a real person, a slave.

This ending has often been criticized. Hemingway calls it a cheat. I don't agree. Something like it is essential to the structure and manner of the book, and there are a number of reasons why it is as it is. The one important to my argument now is that Twain uses the opening and closing Tom Sawyer scenes as a frame for Huck's story. He is in fact setting up the conventional kind of story written for young people in his day, the Tom Sawyer kind, and in Huck's story showing, first, how it is all lies, and, second, how a story can be told so that it incorporates the truth about life while at the same time being a grand adventure that will hit the young reader where s/he lives.

The first chapters of *Huckleberry Finn* set up the conventional action-packed hero fantasy, then Twain uses it against itself, till at the end it descends into farce. That is the importance of the final Tom Sawyer episode. After two hundred pages of Huck's truth, Tom Sawyer's game of let's pretend is ridiculous. A clichéd form is fashioned by Twain into something thoughtful and refreshed. Superficial readers like Tom Sawyer are taken on at their own game and are given the chance of becoming readers with a deepened sense of reality. Adolescence is depicted through its own eyes and enabled to think honestly about itself. Adults are observed with a clarity which is critical yet compassionate—a quality most young adult fiction still has to acquire. The key is Twain's way of telling: in the absorption of his second self, the implied author, into the protagonist and narrator of the book, Huck Finn; and in his management of form.

Huckleberry Finn trusts adolescents with the truth. It doesn't duck the realities of life but acknowledges, indeed reveals, how "sometimes people do get hurt" and how all too often it is "enough to make a body ashamed of the human race." But it is not afraid of the loving, the delicate, the beautiful aspects of life. And because of its irony and the variety of its humour, it maintains throughout a tone of entirely unsentimental optimism. The last thing it is, in other words, is phony or life diminishing. True, it doesn't deal with sex, which might be thought a significant lack these days. But that has to do with the history of its time, just like its handling of Jim's speech; and just as our endless preoccupation with sex has to do with the history of our time and might well seem unbalanced in a hundred years from now. No time is without its stupidities, no book is without flaw. But the flaws in Twain's novel have as much to teach us as do its strengths. Though I should add from not a little experience, anyone trying to live up to the standards set by Twain will certainly find him/herself saying with Huck Finn, "if I'd a knowed what a trouble it was to make a book I wouldn't a tackled it."

At the start I did not intend talking so much about *Huckleberry Finn*, and here I am unable to stop! Which only goes to prove once again that a sign of a great piece of literature, or I suppose of any work of art, is that you become entangled in it and can't shake yourself free. It first captures and then captivates you. The more you say about it, the more there is left to say. Every time you turn to face it, hoping, so to speak, to stare it out, you discover something new you hadn't found before, something fascinating that binds you to it even more firmly. Sooner or later, you realize that you don't want to be free of it, after all, that you love it and find it inexhaustible, a constant source of pleasure, of surprise, and of sustenance: a breeding place of energy and thought. Finally you discover that the truth is a paradox: being captive in the *work* of literature enables you to live your life more freely.

References

1. Patricia Meyer Spacks, *The Adolescent Idea: Myths of Youth and the Adult Imagination* (New York: Basic Books, 1981), p.45.
2. Ibid., p.90.
3. Ibid., p.293.
4. Ibid., p.296.

5. T. S. Eliot, Introduction to Samuel L. Clemens (Mark Twain), *The Adventures of Huckleberry Finn* (London: Cresset Press, 1950), p.vii.
6. Justin Kaplan, *Mr. Clemens and Mark Twain: A Biography,* (London: Johnathan Cape, 1967), p.180.
7. Lionel Trilling, "Huckleberry Finn," in *The Liberal Imagination: Essays on Literature and Society* (Harmondsworth: Penguin, 1970), p.114.
8. Mark Twain, *Huckleberry Finn* (Harmondsworth: Penguin, 1953), p.11. All quotations from the novel are taken from this edition.
9. Lionel Trilling, "Huckleberry Finn," p.117.
10. Quoted in Justin Kaplan, *Born to Trouble: One Hundred Years of Huckleberry Finn*, (Washington, D.C.: Library of Congress, 1985), p.11.
11. Adrian Mitchell, Letter to the editor, *The Listener*, (London: British Broadcasting Corp., January 16, 1986).
12. Quoted in *Ernest Hemingway On Writing*, Ed. by Larry W. Phillips, (London: Granada, 1985), p.93.
13. Mark Twain, *The Adventures of Tom Sawyer* (Harmondsworth: Penguin, 1950), p.14,15.
14. Ibid., p.19.
15. Virginia Hamilton, *The People Could Fly: American Black Folktales* (New York: Random, 1985, and London: Walker Books, 1986), p.5.

James Houston

A Primitive View of the World

James Houston

is a Canadian author of books for children and adults, an artist, a designer and a filmmaker. He is a three-time recipient of the Canadian Library Association's Book of the Year for Children Award for *Tikta'Liktak* (Harcourt, 1965); *The White Archer* (Harcourt, 1967); and *River Runners* (Atheneum, 1979). *The White Archer* was the 1967 Australian Book of the Year. Houston illustrates each of his books, many of which are ALA Notable Children's Books. He is known internationally for his many efforts to preserve and promote the arts and cultures of the Inuit peoples.

IT IS ALMOST IMPOSSIBLE FOR ME TO BELIEVE that I am delivering the eighteenth Arbuthnot Lecture. In truth, I should be seated quietly in the audience, trying to learn all I can about children's literature. Without the twenty-four year friendship and guidance of my beloved editor, Margaret K. McElderry, I would probably not be here tonight. We met on Nantucket Island and our first conversation was about *Tikta'liktak, An Eskimo Legend.* Less than a year later, that turned into my first book. It has been clear sailing ever since.

My Canadian upbringing in children's books was about as simple and direct as that of those native storytellers I admire. When I was very young (age five, six, seven) my father made frequent journeys across Canada. His purpose was ostensibly to sell British tweeds. As my mother explained, this was in part a ruse to travel and visit various Indian tribes. After all, at the beginning of the depression how much expensive Scottish yard goods could one sell to the Chipewyan Indians near Churchill or the Haida Indians on the Queen Charlotte Islands in northern British Columbia.

My sister and I adored my father and longed for the night when we would be taken to the train station to welcome him home. We could never understand why our mother would immediately rush us off to bed, saying, "You can see your father in the morning. He's going to be very busy for a while."

Undaunted, we would leap up at 6 a.m. and rush into our parents' bed, displacing our mother as we crowded one on either side of our father. He would give us each a hug, then produce two pairs of delicious-smelling, smoked, moose-hide moccasins, not those with a few beads scattered here and there, but Indian moccasins of museum quality with vamps adorned with rich designs.

Then came the best part. My father would take up his largest pad of order forms, turn it over and start telling us all the unusual Indian things that he had seen. He would draw Sioux pulling toboggans south of Moose Jaw, Saskatchewan, and Sarcee teepees pitched on the plains near Medicine Hat, painted ponies and feathered riders coming to collect their treaty money, which was annually one pound sterling or five dollars for the head of each family, and Tshimshan dancers at a forbidden potlatch on the North Pacific Coast. I didn't care what other children's fathers did because I would never have traded theirs for mine.

Our family had a summer cottage on Lake Simcoe. We had contacts with Ojibwa Indians, for we lived between the reservations of Georgina, Mara and Snake. An old Ojibwa and his daughter taught us to catch

---

Presented March 13, 1987, at Northern Illinois University, DeKalb. The 1987 Arbuthnot Lecture is sponsored by Scott, Foresman and Company in cooperation with the Association for Library Service to Children.

whitefish, harvest wild rice, and look at nature in old-fashioned ways not usually explained to city kids. Our friendship helped prepare me for my future.

When I was eight or nine years old, I caught scarlet fever in Toronto and was quarantined at home for three long weeks. A carbolic sheet was hung across the entrance to my bedroom to keep the germs from jumping at my sister. My parents and relatives gave me lots of handsomely-illustrated books by Edmund Dulac, Arthur Rackham, and N. C. Wyeth. I especially remember *Robin Hood, Treasure Island,* and *King Arthur.*

One afternoon, to my horror, my mother came and said, "Jimmy, give me all your books. A government man is here to burn them so other children won't catch scarlet fever." I was devastated.

Next morning, my mother came into my room and handed me what was to be my only book. I eagerly opened the cover only to find that it was entirely blank—no words, no pictures. My mother smiled, "If you want a book, make one yourself."

I was only eight, but I started to create a story about being shipwrecked, cast away on a small island very different from Robinson Crusoe's. Of course, I did my own illustrations. That drove the scarlet fever away, but that book, like all the others, did not survive.

In the following year, when I was nine, a Canadian magazine offered me the chance to illustrate a poem written by a girl of about my age. It was entitled, "The Boy on the Flying Trapeze." I followed their rules scrupulously, using India ink on a smooth piece of paper that the publisher had sent to me. To my delight three weeks later, on the magazine's front page, was my illustration and the girl's poem.

"Wait! That's not all," my mother said, and out of the package she drew a large green check for three dollars. Wow! I had never had so much money in all my life. She said, "Go and show your uncle."

My uncle knew about money. He managed a bank. When the teller ran in and told my uncle of my good fortune, he hurried out of his office and said, "Jimmy, you must open a penny savings account."

What could I say! Naturally I was wary, knowing that all my Scottish uncles were well-known penny pinchers. He said, "You must keep 25 cents and deposit the rest right here."

I looked at my uncle and I thought, I am never going to be a banker or a lawyer or a doctor or anything respectable like that. I knew then and there that I would draw pictures and maybe learn to write, anything to make an easy joyful living.

Toronto even in those far-off days had some wonderful benefits for children. The Guggenheim Foundation had reached north and through the Toronto Art Gallery offered special training to a few children who could pass their school's art test and then an art gallery competition with all other city students. Fortunately I was accepted. I believe I was eleven and twelve. Every Saturday, as well as Thursday afternoons, I drew and painted.

Blessed was the day when Dr. Arthur Lismer became our teacher there. He was a prominent member of Canada's Group of Seven and one of the country's most famous artists. For some reason, he went away to Africa and, of course, that extraordinary man did not return to us in any ordinary way. He arrived on a Saturday morning amidst wild West African drumming and singing. The recorded music resounded through the galleries as he danced among us, his face hidden by a huge Congo mask. I remember thinking who made that mask, who is beating those exciting rhythms on the drums? I was hooked forever on the lives of primitive people. I trembled to think of my own teacher, Dr. Lismer, treading on the soil of Africa, perhaps paddling on the Congo River with big crocodiles around him. I determined at that moment that I, too, would go to see the wildest corners of the earth.

Seven years later, my father died; it was the beginning of World War II. In 1940, I was old enough to volunteer. I left the Ontario College of Art and served for five years with the Toronto Scottish Regiment.

After the war, I stayed for some time with my Scottish cousin and in late 1947, it was possible to obtain a student's visa to France. I attended L'Ecole Grand Chaumiere in Paris, especially for its life drawing classes, continuing studies that had been interrupted by the war. I had been in Paris for less than a year when my mother wrote me, saying, "I don't know what you are doing over there, but it is making me terribly nervous."

I returned to Montreal and then Toronto. After Paris, both cities struck me as being far too proper, with men in gray baggy suits and girls tightly bound in girdles. I asked myself where should I go?

In 1948, I went and asked the station master in Grandmere, Quebec, what train would carry me furthest north. He looked it up and said, "You can go to Churchill, Manitoba, or to Moosonee, Ontario. Moosonee is cheaper."

I paid the $19 and bought a one-way ticket to Moosonee, taking with me only my sketchbooks, extra clothing, and my sleeping bag. You must remember, that apart from the unpaved Alaska Highway 2,000 miles to the west, there were no roads in northern Canada. At that time only the Hudson Bay Company's ship went in once a year to supply their Arctic posts. Airplanes flew north occasionally, but they were military or charter flights that I could not afford.

When I arrived in Moosonee, then romantically called the "end of steel," the small weekly train made an elaborate turnabout and departed. A young Swampy Cree Indian with a large canoe offered me a free ride to the island where he lived called Moose Factory. The Hudson's Bay Company had established themselves there in the 1670s, a very early date in Canada's history. I remained at Moose Factory drawing Swampy Cree Indians and wondering where my father had slept twenty years earlier.

I stayed as a guest in the old Hudson's Bay staff house, for there was no place else. It was overseen by a jolly factor who was like a father to his flock of lively Scottish clerks, all practicing at this trading post while waiting to be sent out to remote Indian outposts like Kaniapuscow, Beaver House, Nemiscow, Winish, and Great Whale River. My close contacts with HBC traders from then until this day has left a strong impression on me. The Honourable Company of Gentlemen Trading into Hudson Bay, as they call themselves, figures in many of my books.

While making hundreds of drawings of the Cree, who forty years ago still dressed in braids, tartan shawls and knee-high moccasins, I made friends with them and with George Charity, a bush pilot, and Dr. Herbert Harper, the resident surgeon for Indian Health Services.

One morning early, the day before I planned to return south, George Charity burst into my small room and said, "If you'll help me woggle the gas, you can fly into the Arctic with us—free! We're leaving now! The doctor has an emergency."

I was up, dressed and pumping gas into that old single-engine Norseman before anyone could gulp down a cup of coffee.

As we flew north, the doctor explained what had happened. A hunter had come into the trading post at Inukjuak to say that a woman in their camp had heard dogs stealing food in the porchlike front of her family tent. When bending over to drive off the hungry dogs, they had leapt up and snatched from her hood the baby she was carrying. The mother had fought to get her child back and had succeeded, but it was badly bitten and so was she. Inukjuak had sent word of the emergency to Moose Factory by Morse code, for there was nothing so modern between those two remote places as voice transmission. The doctor reckoned we might stay about four days. He would stitch up the child, give it penicillin, and make sure it was recovering before we journeyed south again.

Flying along the east coast of Hudson Bay, I watched the spruce trees thin, and as we crossed the wide sweep of Great Whale River, they disappeared beneath us. Beyond it were large patches of green caribou moss and then only rocks and autumn tundra turning red before the snows. We found the hunting camp beyond Inukjuak, and our float plane came coughing in for a landing.

The doctor, when we beached, was led to the right tent by a crowd of Inuit-Eskimo. We anchored the aircraft and I got out my sketchbook and prepared to draw. I had never been so excited in all my life. Out on Hudson Bay, long skeins of ice were drifting south from the Foxe Basin. Behind me, the treeless tundra rolled endlessly to the skyline. But best of all, crowding around me were short, sturdy, dark-tanned Inuit, laughing, flashing their white teeth as they spoke Inuktitut, a rich and complex language of which, like everyone else, I knew two words: *igloo* and *kayak*.

In less time than it takes to tell, the doctor came running out of the tent with the child in his arms, the mother following. "Come on right now. We're leaving. I don't know how this child is still alive."

Leaving! I could scarcely believe the word. I had barely set pencil to paper and felt certain this chance would never come again.

"I am staying," I said.

"Staying?" he yelled. "How can you stay here? What will your mother say?"

Finally the plane flew off and I remained, beginning a great personal adventure which still goes on.

Not long after I arrived at that northern camp, a man named

Naiomialook came and held out his closed fist. When he opened his hand, he revealed a small stone carving of a bear. Of course, I had seen such objects in museums, and I assumed this one might be a family heirloom, the work of his great-grandfather, or possibly much older. It had the robust character of a Neolithic figure. I was overwhelmed.

Pleased by my reaction, he took me to his tent and showed me two more carvings, one of which was ivory. I journeyed with great excitement to the nearest Hudson's Bay Company trader, a friendly Scot of wide Arctic experience. I showed him the carvings and asked how old he thought they were. He said they were probably carved at least a week ago!

Some might have thought that disappointing. I found it super-exciting to think that such amazing art was being created here and now.

I was just beginning my struggles with the language and if I couldn't act out a question, my sketchbooks often saved me. When I needed to communicate, I could usually make some kind of drawing, or some Inuk would take my book from me and sketch an explanation. I drew them and they in turn with utter confidence drew me. Much of the language I acquired was from their children. In summer tents or winter igloos, they would jump on my chest in the early morning and teach me dozens of useful words. My struggle to learn the language continued over four and a half years. When I could speak it reasonably well, I was always eager to use it.

None of those far northern people at that time relied upon the written word to convey their delights or fears of their astonishing and sometimes magical world. They used that age-old art of oral storytelling which involves the breathtaking excitement of the human voice mixed with animal sounds and shouts often accompanied by dancing and the rhythm of the drum or the howling Arctic winds. Sometimes the storyteller's helper clicked a goose quill against his teeth to help build excitement and suspense. A good northern storyteller revealed through many a means the agility and cunning of the bear, the huge bulk of fearlessness of walrus, the beauty in the flight of geese, the tenderness of a mother to a child, or perhaps the mystical gaze of the moon.

Storytelling was just one of many Inuit arts. There were, of course, no special stories for children. Every modern story, myth or legend was told to suit all ages. The Wolf Dance of the King Island Eskimos in Alaska takes four days and nights to perform. It is a great saga accompanied by hypnotic beating of drums and many songs and tales.

In Canada's Arctic, storytelling differed slightly. Drumming was consciously used to create a hypnotic effect as was the ancient women's habit of throat singing, a process that may be accomplished in several ways. The custom began with two unmarried women who would place their mouths together, then, in turn or in rhythm, blow on each other's vocal cords to create a uniquely haunting sound.

Shamen had the power, so they say, to leap upon a single drumbeat and ride it into the other world. *Shamen* were hired with gifts of clothing, food, and shelter to journey into the spirit world to discover why the hunting has failed or a grandparent was ailing. Once in a dance house at Ennadia

Lake, I watched the audience swaying, mesmerized by hours of steady, repetitious drumming.

Inuit songs and stories, like their carvings often reveal an enormous freshness and ingenuity. But there is one enormous difference. A carving may be lost in the permafrost near some ancient campsite only to be excavated thousands of years later to tell us much about its maker. An unrecorded story or a song will disappear forever with the last breath of its teller and has no way to return.

How many myths and songs like these must have been lost?

Ayii, Ayii,
The great sea has set me in motion,
Set me adrift,
And I move as a weed in the river.
The arch of sky
And mightiness of storms
Encompasses me,
And I am left
Trembling with joy.

And a second one:

Ayii, Ayii,
I walked on the ice of the sea.
Wondering, I heard
The song of the sea
And the great sighing
Of new formed ice.
Go then go!
Strength of soul
Brings health
To the place of feasting.

As an observer who would one day write stories, how could I have dared to dream of any better opportunity than listening to their day-by-day adventures and their myths and legends of the past?

I soon discovered that among the Inuit one was not at liberty to tell someone else's story, which was considered personal property and, in a sense, copyrighted. Finally I realized that if I wished to have a story to tell, I would have to trade for it, giving sugar, tea, rifle bullets, and flour. I carefully practiced all the words, but found that my listeners who sat on the wide bed began to tip over and fall sound asleep.

About that time, I made a long dog team journey with a biologist from Edinburgh University who wished to study Baffin Island caribou. Later, when we had circled to Kingmeruk, we spent a night or so with a Scottish trader. We had been completely out of touch, and I was anxious to hear world news from his radio. I heard for the first time that the Russians had launched a satellite named Sputnik, that it had flown around the world in space and had a dog inside. Wow! What news! Next morning, Oshaweetok, my traveling companion, asked if I had heard anything interesting on the radio, the *nalautik.* In my mind, I had all the words in place to tell what I had heard and I repeated to him in Inuktitut the story about the enormous bullet named Sputnik (an Eskimo-sounding word) that had flown around the world with a dog inside.

"You mean the dog was doing the driving, just sitting driving? *Wahkudlunga!*" Oshaweetok shouted. "If anybody tries to buy that story from you, you sell it for a lot!"

To define the difference between legends and myths I went to Webster and the *OED*. Both sources agree that a legend is a story coming down from the historical past but is not verifiable. A myth is a person or thing existing only in the imagination.

The reason Inuit have found it necessary to mythicize a true event so quickly is, I believe, because their hunting society, to survive, was forced to remain small and scattered. By small I mean perhaps twenty-five seminomadic persons living and moving together in an annual round of their forefathers' hunting places. True events were altered to avoid ordinary recognition, but young people were expected to hear and remember oral myths and carry that knowledge into future generations.

For example, it is known that one man stabbed another in an argument about who should have a certain woman for a wife. The families of those two hunters and the woman were so close that this shocking event could never be discussed without offending one family or the other, thus inviting a feud. So a clever storyteller created a myth and a song, turning those three humans into animals: a wolf, a raven, and a snow bunting. Still that myth survived, was widely told and handed down. This is the oral tradition at its best.

It seems to me that most Inuit legends will not translate directly into the kind of stories that our children or adults would find acceptable because the legends follow a very ancient form. They require no real beginning or ending as we understand them. The stories usually are told with the assumption that every listener possesses all local knowledge—of humans, animals, and seasonal conditions—and are ended bluntly, without seeming to have reached any recognizable conclusion.

Here is an Arctic legend that our archaeologists are still constructing, based on unverifiable truths. About 16,000 years ago, the glacier that had spread over most of northern Europe started to recede and following it went those animals that were built for cold and that grazed on tundra mosses: hairy mammoths, musk-oxen, wolves, caribou and wild ponies. The Neolithic hunters had drawn them on the walls of the caves of Lascaux, France and Altamira, Spain, and in Hungary as well. After that, these ancient artist-hunters followed their quarry north to the Arctic Ocean where they probably learned to hunt out on the frozen sea. Then, after a journey that must have taken thousands of years, they turned east toward the rising sun and crossed into America. This recent migration had nothing to do with the much earlier Indian crossing, as much as 40,000 years ago, on a land bridge when it existed between Asia and America. The Eskimo migration is believed to have occurred 5,000 years ago and less, when those nomadic hunters crossed from Asia, a distance of only twenty miles on water. They used small craft or walked over on the ice.

Eskimo art is astonishingly similar to the work of those Neolithic people from European caves. The language of Inuktitut has no Oriental basis. Its roots are in Hungarian Magyar and the ancient Finno-Ugrian language. South to north, then east, would seem to mark the path of that early migration. Our Alaskan-Canadian Eskimos left several thousand relatives behind in Asia as if to mark the route of their ancient journey.

Originally, in almost all native legends, the world was flat. Inuit-Eskimo usually described its edges as being hidden in ice fog. It was said that travelers could and did sometimes fall off. The sky was held up by four huge carved wooden posts.

Television and schooling have spoiled all that, for now the children see classroom globes, and the elder Arctic viewers see our round world spinning most every night during the introduction to the news program.

An anthropologist asked an old storyteller, "Whatever happened to that flat world of yours?"

The man answered, "Well, it was certainly flat when I was young, but then you people blew it up with that great bang and spreading cloud. You curled up the world like a ball of dried seaweed. I don't know how we're ever going to get it flat again."

Imagine the differences that have occurred in 40 years! Arctic settlements are now decorated by satellite dishes delivering wide-screen color television. In the eastern regions, where so few can understand English or French, it means that real events on the evening news cannot be separated from ficticious programs such as *Hill Street Blues*. All our truths, myths, legends, wars and violence are mixed together without any interpretation. No wonder so few Inuit would choose to risk their lives here in the South among us.

The story of Sedna is one of the Arctic's great classic myths. This traditional song goes with it.

Ayii, Ayii, Ayii.
That woman down there beneath the sea,
She wants to hide the seals from us.
These hunters in the dance house
They cannot mend matters.
They cannot change matters.
Into the spirit world
Will go I,
Where no humans dwell.
Set matters right will I.
Set matters right will I.
Ayii, Ayii, Ayii.

Sedna became a sea goddess, half seal, half woman, but that was not always so. The last part of the saga is best known, when she was sacrificed by her father and other hunters to save their own lives.

It is the first and least-known part of the myth that interests me. Sedna was said to be a loving young girl, a joy to all her family. In summer she wandered with them over the inland in search of caribou; in winter they hunted out on the frozen sea.

One night during a blizzard, they heard a dog team arrive and into their igloo came a handsome young man. He wore beautifully fitted skin clothing with a curious amulet around his neck bearing two large white canine teeth.

After Sedna's father had shared food with this bright-eyed stranger, the family made space for him in the center of the family bed and slept. In the morning, the stranger was gone, leaving no sign that he had been there. The father went out and searched but found no sled tracks. When he returned to the igloo, he said, "I believe that was no human who slept here. It was my lead dog. He's just sly enough to pull off a trick like that."

Moons passed, summer came and Sedna said that she was pregnant.

"He did it!" shouted the father and went out to give his lead dog a good swift kick.

"I am worried about what she may produce," the father told the mother. "Will it be like us or perhaps a litter of pups? What will the other families say? Daughter, lie on the back of my kayak. I am going to paddle you out to that small rocky island. You can give birth there."

Sedna would surely have died of hunger, but the lead dog swam to the island, bringing meat to her every other day.

When Sedna did give birth, half of the six young born were clearly humans and the other three had big ears, doglike snouts and whined instead of crying. Sedna could not build a proper boat, but the lead dog brought her three sealskins, and she sewed these into one large boatlike slipper. Sadly she placed the doglike creatures in it and when the tide was running out, she pushed them southward, crying, "You shall be clever at making weapons."

That is why Inuit when first seeing us often cry out, "Welcome, cousins. You return."

During the dark month of November, 1986, I returned to Baffin Island, though not for the first time, of course, hopping around by air for the Canada Council and the territorial government. It was a wonderful opportunity for me to see Inuit cousins and their children again. Some I had seen recently, but others I had not seen for twenty, even thirty, years. What would I say to them? My usual talks are about Inuit or northern Indians. I couldn't go up and tell them about themselves!

Still, I had to say something. Dare I tell them how our folk live in hot, southern places like Ottawa or Chicago? Lord, no! That would be far too risky. So we talked about the good old days instead.

To my delight I found Inuit school children reading most of my books, legends I had written years before. I never imagined the children reading English or my books staying in print that long. I spoke of *Kiviok's Magic Journey,* the only myth I ever wrote, and *The White Archer,* a legend that the students knew. They especially liked *Frozen Fire,* in which I wrote of a real event where an Inuk boy was lost on moving ice and of how he survived. I coupled that with a second core of truth about a boy from the south, his father, and a search for precious metals, using a helicopter. That book has been by far my most popular children's book, along with *Black Diamonds* and *Ice Swords,* which complete the trilogy.

The film rights to an adult novel of mine entitled *The White Dawn* were purchased by Paramount Pictures. In 1973, the producers offered me the chance to write the screenplay and later work as associate producer in the Arctic. Obviously no one from Hollywood can have wanted the job!

That story was based on a true event which had taken place seventy-five years earlier. We filmed on Baffin Island with Inuit actors playing the parts of their own forebears. The whole process of making the movie greatly interested the local people, and they supplied many rich details.

In the final scene, when the young New England whaler from the South is executed by a hunter's arrows, the whole impact of their legend returned to them, and many Inuit women who were watching cried out, "Wrong! Wrong to kill that boy!"

This reaction was typical of their compassion for all living things.

Another example is in the story that tells how a long time ago, a mosquito landed on a boy's ear. The boy drew back his hand to strike. "Don't hit, don't hit," whined the mosquito. "I still have unsung songs to pass on to my grandchildren."

"Imagine that," said the boy, "one so small and yet a grandfather!"

I believe having a direct living experience with the culture about which one is writing is invaluable. This has long been my method of relating northern stories, and I believe it would apply to other cultures around the world. After ten years of living part of every year near the Haida, I only now consider writing about them.

Taping or copying down some oral legend directly from the mouth of a native narrator and guiding it verbatim into print is properly the task of an anthropologist. But scientific papers rarely make exciting children's reading. A story must first be a good story, whether it is part of a children's book or an adult novel, and an author must not be tempted to let too many facts get in the way. Authors of books for children have the challenge of combining fact and fiction in fascinating ways.

Authors have imaginative works to do. I feel one should listen carefully to what indigenous people have to say about their lives, hear what they value or perhaps disdain, and try to understand their traditions and customs, and, indeed, their legends. Finally you may hear a core of truth, something that excited them and has the same effect on you. As William Blake has written in the "Proverbs" from the *Marriage of Heaven and Hell,* "One thought fills immensity."

After twelve years, I left Baffin Island, where my administration was spread over an area of 65,000 square miles. Humans there were separated into fifty-eight families living in thirteen camps having a total population, at the time, of 341 persons. That population has now more than doubled itself.

I landed in the steamy heart of Manhattan, where a much larger population might live in many moderate-sized apartment buildings. It was much more of a cultural shock than I anticipated. Remember, I used to receive mail once a year by icebreaker and answer it only in the following year. What an ideal job for any federal civil servant!

I did adjust to life in Manhattan and lived there for nine years designing for Steuben Glass. I came to enjoy living in that great city of libraries, art galleries, museums, windows, and faces. But I must confess that I have always managed to escape back to the joys of the eastern Arctic or the north Pacific coast, where my wife and I have a writing and fishing cottage. I am still grateful I did not become a banker. Writing and drawing are for me an enormous pleasure.

After living twenty-five years of adult life in Canada and that same length of time in the United States, I find no very special difference. Together we inhabit a truly breathtaking continent. I wish we as countries could join together and more closely share our common destinies.

When today's great carvers and storytellers disappear, will their children carry on the culture? I believe so, based on the traditions and talents of the young people. Inuit have never been so threatened as they are today by our juggernaut of civilization. But remember, we are dealing with the world's hardiest survivors. They are only now becoming deeply concerned about us.

John Bierhorst

Pushing Up the Sun a Little

John Bierhorst

is a scholar, collector, editor and translator of North and South American Indian literature and a specialist in the language of the Aztecs. His numerous scholarly publications for adults are recognized as reliable by many, as are his books for children, which include these named as ALA Notable Children's Books: *In the Trail of the Wind; American Indian Poems and Ritual Orations* (Farrar, 1971); *Black Rainbow; Legends of the Incas and Myths of Ancient Peru* (Farrar, 1976); *The Girl Who Married a Ghost, and Other Tales from the North American Indian* (Four Winds, 1978); *A Cry from the Earth; Music of the North American Indians* (Four Winds, 1979); *The Whistling Skeleton; American Indian Tales of the Supernatural* (Four Winds, 1982); *The Sacred Path; Spells, Prayers and Power Songs of the American Indians* (Morrow, 1983); and *Spirit Child; A Story of the Nativity* (Morrow, 1984). The jacket and text designs of Bierhorst's books are created by his wife, Jane Byers Bierhorst, and are often cited for excellence.

I WANT TO THANK the American Library Association for asking me to give this talk in the Arbuthnot series and my friends at the University of Oklahoma for offering to be the host.

Looking back over the published Arbuthnot lectures, which began in 1970, I have the feeling that they are becoming an organic work—somewhat in the manner of a Japanese *renga,* or linked verse, to which each of several participants adds a new stanza; or like one of those Eskimo narrative sessions where each teller ends by saying to the next person, "You can't leave it standing on one leg." In the case at hand the unifying theme turns out to be children's literature around the world, and the story thus far has touched every continent except Africa, coming in from nations as diverse as Japan, Israel, and Canada. This does not seem to have been planned. But it is true that the stimulus of other lands and other peoples has been an activating force among educators, librarians, and publishers throughout the modern history of books for children—as part of the idealism that we project on younger generations; they are our hope for a more perfect world.

Those of us who grew up in the 1940s, as I did, will recall that the theme was given fresh impetus by the horror of World War II and the establishment of the United Nations in 1945. May Hill Arbuthnot's monumental *Children and Books* appeared in 1947. This was the work that prepared the way for subsequent scholarship in the field of children's reading; and the book's attempt to encompass the literature of the entire world was unmistakable.

But by the early 1960s it was becoming clear that the world was even larger than some people had thought, or at least it was not getting smaller. In the United States, people of European descent began to realize that ethnic groups that were supposed to have melted or, in the case of the American Indian, vanished, had somehow resisted the so-called American melting pot. To its credit, children's literature took up the challenge, and books began to appear that were sensitive to the needs of black, Asian, Latin American, and Native American children, not only as individuals but as members of their respective cultural groups.

Among social scientists the doctrine of cultural relativism had already been articulated a generation earlier. As Margaret Mead and other anthropologists had expressed it, all cultures, regardless of military or technological prowess, are equal in dignity; or, as formulated by Ruth Benedict in her elegant *Patterns of Culture,* each people's way of life amounts to a work of art. Such a doctrine goes beyond the comfortable idea that all human beings are brothers and sisters, because it implies that not only human lives but life styles, group values, and group attitudes are to be respected.

Presented April 9, 1988, at the University of Oklahoma at Norman. The 1988 Arbuthnot Lecture is sponsored by Scott, Foresman and Company in cooperation with the Association for Library Service to Children.

When mainstream America, including the world of children's books, finally caught up with relativism in the 1960s and 1970s, there were objections, at first feeble, but eventually strenuous. Within Anthropology itself the doctrine came to be reexamined by those who saw a need to assert *basic* human values, free of culture. Ironically, one of those basic values may turn out to be tolerance for different styles of life.

In such a climate the writer or editor who brings news from one culture to another enjoys a heightened sense of purpose. There are readers who care deeply about what is being written. At the same time there are demanding requirements for sensitivity and, above all, authenticity. With as little interference as possible on the part of the translator or presenter, there is a need to hear authentic stories, poetry, songs, and first-person accounts—because the essence of a culture is best conveyed in the words of the people who have lived it.

Tonight I would like to share with you a case in point, out of my own experience in the literatures of native America. I would like you to join me in taking a close look at childhood in a particular culture, the literature available to its children, and the problems and opportunities in bringing that literature to children whose language is English.

The culture I have in mind was developed by a people who spoke the language we now call Classical Nahuatl. Their capital was eleven hundred miles south of the University of Oklahoma—not so far as one might think, in fact considerably less than the extent of the Inca empire of Peru, which once spanned twenty-five hundred miles. Their own empire, at the time of the first contact with Europeans, had been rapidly expanding, with outposts on both the western and eastern oceans. If Columbus had not set sail, or if his voyage had been delayed by several hundred years, it is possible that I would be speaking to you this evening in their language, just as Latin, the language of the Roman empire, was used in the academies of Europe until only recently. In that event I would open with this greeting: *oannechmocnelilique ma ximonenemitican,* "You have favored me, may you live."

The culture of the people who spoke this language—we call them Aztecs—may be viewed dispassionately, perhaps, because it has passed into history. Or, to use the Nahuatl expression, "its years are complete." But this is not to say that the Aztecs do not have the power to stir memories. Native North Americans continue to identify with Montezuma, the last of the Aztec emperors, and to draw inspiration from the Aztec god-man Quetzalcoatl. And today, many Mexican-Americans are using the term Aztlan, the name of the legendary Aztec homeland, when referring to that portion of the United States taken from Mexico around 1850, the so-called Southwest, stretching from Texas and western Oklahoma to the Pacific Ocean. In fact I am addressing you tonight at the frontier of Aztlan. So we may say that Aztec culture continues to operate in people's minds.

Among the Aztecs, childhood—life itself—began when the mother reached what was spoken of as her "moment of death." As soon as she felt the first labor pains, the midwife quickly washed her, placed her in a sweating room, and had her drink an infusion of the herb called woman medicine. As the baby came forth, the midwife shouted, uttering a war cry, a sign that the mother had won her battle.

When the umbilical cord had been cut, the midwife and her attendants bathed the newborn and presented the infant with a broom, a spindle, and a sewing basket, if the child were female; if male, a miniature shield and four little arrows. For a girl the umbilical cord was buried in the house, next to the hearth, to show that her future place would be in the home. For a boy, the cord was wrapped around the shield and the arrows and given to warriors, who were charged with burying it in a distant battlefield.

This assumes that the child has been born on a lucky day according to the calendar—for example, 1 Alligator, in which case the elder relatives would say, "The child has reached the earth on 1 Alligator. Let it be bathed." But if the birth occurred, say, on 6 Dog, a day comparable to Friday the thirteenth in European lore, the baby's ritual bath would be postponed until a more favorable date came around.

As part of the ceremony the child was given its name and placed in its cradle. Members of the family prepared feast foods, and the guests who arrived brought flowers. After a long speech of greeting had been addressed to the child, everyone petted the infant, stroking it with their hands to show their love. Speeches were also addressed to the mother, warning her not to pull the child away from her breast too abruptly, for fear of tearing the baby's palate; and to be careful, while sleeping, not to roll over and crush the child.

Thereafter, according to the sixteenth-century missionary, Fray Toribio de Benavente, the child was given "four years of milk." "And," he tells us, "these people loved their children so much and raised them with so much love that the mother, to keep from hurting her child by becoming pregnant with another one, would assiduously avoid the attentions of her husband." In the words of Fray Diego de Durán, another of the early missionaries, the Aztecs were "the people who loved their children more than any other nation in the world."

The most authoritative of the missionary ethnographers, Fray Bernardino de Sahagún, who recorded the actual Nahuatl expressions and figures of speech, put it this way: in Aztec families children were said to be "pushing up the sun a little"; by contrast it was said that the mature person "puts the sun at the zenith," while for the elderly the sun was "setting." Contemplating a child, old people would say, "This is our blessing, this is our reward," or "This pushes up the sun a little."

Sometime during the first four years of life the child's ears would be pierced. The age varied because the ear-piercing ceremony could be held only at four-year intervals. On this occasion the children received godparents, a so-called aunt and uncle for each child. When the time came, the parents presented gifts to the prospective "aunts" and "uncles," the children's ears were pierced with an awl—while they squirmed—and a cotton thread was drawn through the opening and bound in place temporarily. Later, an ornament, or signet, would be inserted, by which the godparent would recognize the child. Also at this time, adults went from child to child, picking up each one by the head, as if to stretch, or lengthen, the body. This was to insure that the child would grow tall—a custom still observed in some parts of Mexico. The ceremony ended with wine drinking, for young and old alike. Children were allowed to sip the wine from tiny cups, and even babies still in their cradles were given a bit of foot moistened with the wine. For this reason people often referred to the ceremony as The Children's Wine-drinking.

Participation in adult activities was a prominent theme throughout the years of childhood. Adult choirs included boy sopranos; on certain occasions when adults danced, children danced with them; if feathers were worn by the dancers, the children also wore them, and even babies in their cradles were adorned with a few plumes; on holidays children were expected to make offerings and burn incense; and when a new baby received its name, the name was told first to a group of waiting children, who rushed into the streets to cry it through the town.

Age five or six marked a turning point. By this time the child had finally been weaned and, being able to run, could be sent out to play. But there were chores to be done as well; and if a game were interrupted and could not be finished, someone might announce to the others, with resignation: "Let's just say a little mouse drank it up." A boy, then, might be asked to fetch wood or a load of straw. Or he might be sent to the marketplace to pick up scraps of corn or beans that had been left by the merchants. For a girl it might be a beginning lesson in spinning or weaving.

Even at so early an age girls were taught to comport themselves with the dignity and modesty befitting young maidenhood. Nevertheless, a little girl was permitted to have chewing gum. If a boy wanted to chew gum, he had to do it secretly. And then, if a tooth fell out, the mother would say to the child, "Put it in a mousehole." Otherwise, it was believed, the permanent tooth would not come in.

The ideal child was the child who obeyed. In the words of an elder, the model boy was "obedient, humble, gracious, grateful, reverent . . . thankful, appreciative." The good daughter was said to be "obedient, honest, intelligent, discreet, of good memory, modest, respectful, revered, well reared, well taught, well trained, well instructed, prudent, chaste, circumspect."

At age ten, said to be the "age of discretion," there came a second turning point. At ten, children were considered legally responsible for their misdemeanors and could be sentenced to punishment. By now, or by age thirteen at the latest, all boys and girls had been enrolled in boarding schools, where discipline was a way of life.

Often the punishments were imaginative. An unruly boy, for instance, could be made to inhale the acrid fumes from a fire to which chili peppers had been added. A wayward girl could be punished by having thorns pressed into her feet or by having her feet tied together.

The schools were of two basic types: the temple schools, which were exceedingly strict, and the somewhat more relaxed neighborhood schools. The children slept and boarded at these institutions, even though they were within walking distances of their homes. Girls and boys were educated separately.

At the temple schools hard work, discipline, and chastity were the watchwords. Girls were sequestered behind high walls and were admonished to keep their eyes lowered. There was no conversation at mealtimes and no idle conversation at any time. For such a remark as "I hear a drum, I wonder where they're dancing," a girl could be severely punished. For greater chastity, so it was said, the girls slept fully clothed. Similarly, in the priests' schools, boys slept separately; no two boys were covered by the same blanket.

On the other hand, a glimpse of life at the eminently practical featherworkers' school, located in the featherworking district, shows us young people busily learning to paste, cut, weave, and embroider, with the youngest children stirring the glue pots.

Generally speaking, the more intellectual labors were performed at the temple schools, where students learned music, history, rhetoric, the art of painting books, the use of the calendar, and the interpretation of dreams. At least some of these subjects, especially music, were also taught at the neighborhood schools. An effort was made to direct children toward the kind of education for which they were best suited. A boy with a priestly bent, even if he had started at a neighborhood school, could be switched to a temple school.

A third turning point came at the age of fifteen or sixteen. By now the boy was ready to be either a priest or a warrior in training; and the girl, if she did not choose to become a priestess, was ready for marriage. Thus the years of childhood and puberty came to a definitive end.

Aztec culture and its transmission from one generation to the next depended upon the authority of the parent and the vulnerability of the child; during the years immediately following the Spanish Conquest this state of affairs was reversed—it was turned on its head—and in the process Aztec literature as we know it today came into existence.

Seizing upon the children as the most promising candidates for conversion, Franciscan missionaries as early as the 1520s swept them into special schools, where they were instructed in Latin and Spanish and given catechism. In addition they were taught to write and read the Nahuatl language using alphabetic script, with the idea that they would bring Christian doctrine back to their home communities, becoming in effect the teachers of their own elders. If the parents were caught backsliding, the children reported this to the friars. And in fact there were cases of recalcitrant parents who were bodily tied and carried to the monastery for religious instruction.

In order to learn about the old religion, so that it could be more effectively replaced by the new, the friars began interviewing the older people, taking down the texts of songs, histories, and other lore, using their young students as scribes. In time the students on their own, fascinated by the old culture, recorded further texts—until before long an entire literature had grown up.

Looking back, we recognize this as the first written literature of the native New World. Today, of course, it is by no means alone. In the late twentieth century we also pay homage to the significant written and oral literatures of the Cheyenne, the Pawnee, the Creek, the Arapaho, and the Cherokee—to name a few—whose inheritors are here in Oklahoma;

just as we honor the modern writings in English of such Oklahomans as the Kiowa novelist N. Scott Momaday or the Creek poet Joy Harjo. All of this is Indian literature. And—in its *written* form—it begins with Classical Nahuatl.

What did these children, these young students of four hundred and fifty years ago, help to preserve?

First, there are the ritual orations, or *huehuetlatolli,* the elegant speeches contrived for every occasion, whether the address is to fellow humans or supernatural powers. Notice the rhetorical couplets, the triplet, and the repeated naming in this excerpt from the oration to the goddess of water, Jade Skirt, delivered by the midwife as she gives the newborn baby her first bath:

May her heart
  her life
become good
    perfect
    pure
so that she may live beautifully
  calmly on earth . . .
she is in your hands, O noble one
    our great one
    Jade Woman
    Jade Skirt
    Jade-that-shines
    mother of gods
    sister of gods
the child has been left in your hands.[1]

These *huehuetlatolli* form a monumental corpus of Nahuatl rhetoric that has come to be translated and analyzed only recently. The principle source is a manuscript known as the Florentine Codex, prepared by Sahagún and his Indian students.

Next, we have what is commonly referred to as Aztec poetry—really the words to songs whose melodies have been lost. These, for the most part, are on the subject of war and the uncertainty of life. But here are the words to a mother's lullaby, addressed to the infant king Ahuitzotl:

Little jewel, stop crying you little
  babe, I'll lay you in your cradle,
  little Ahuitzotl, your father will
  come, he will rock you.
My heart enjoys it, I've made you, my
  little babe, little Ahuitzotl, your
  father will come, he will rock
  you.[2]

Written down in the sixteenth century, the lullaby for Ahuitzotl—with its emphasis on the father's return—is a typical American Indian cradlesong. Notice its resemblance to this modern Creek lullaby from Oklahoma:

Baby, sleep, sleep, sleep
Father has gone to find turtle shells
He said he will be back tomorrow
Baby, sleep, sleep, sleep.[3]

The Aztec lullaby, no doubt, goes back to pre-Conquest times. But many of the song texts that have been preserved were composed after the Spaniards had arrived. These often show Christian influence, as does this poetic version of the Creation story from the Book of Genesis, which I here translate from the Nahuatl:

God says it, and he creates it: first
  was the light. And on the second
  day he made the sky.
The third day he makes the ocean and
  also the land. And the fourth day
  he establishes the sun. Oh, and
  the moon and all the stars.
On the fifth day the water creatures
  were made, then all the birds that
  fly along.
The sixth day our Lord made the wild
  beasts and all the living things on
  earth, and at that time he created
  the first human being. "Ah, let it
  be so. My very likeness, my very
  image shall be made. This is the
  one who will rule the earth."[4]

Both the lullaby and the Creation song are preserved in the codex Cantares Mexicanos, the principal source of Aztec poetry, apparently compiled by the Indian students of Sahagún, working on their own.

Aztec literature also includes magic spells, which are remarkably similar to the *idi:gawé:sdi,* or incantations, of the Oklahoma Cherokees. These are short, verbal formulas calculated to make a garden grow, cure a sick child, appease anger, or put someone to sleep. Here, for example, are words uttered by a young man who wishes to attract a young woman:

Now! I am a young warrior.
I shine, I dawn . . .
Will I find her tomorrow? The next day? Now!
I am a young warrior![5]

Both the immediacy and the imagery of this magic spell may be compared to one of the many Cherokee incantations used by young men to attract women:

Now! I am as beautiful as the very
blossoms themselves!
I am a man, you lovely ones, you women
  of the Seven Clans! . . .
All of you have just come to gaze upon

me alone, the most beautiful.
Now! You lovely women, already I just
took your souls!
I am a man![6]

And like the Cherokees, the Aztecs wrote their spells on little slips of paper so that they would not forget the exact words. The great collectors of the *idi:gawé:sdi* were the late Jack and Anna Kilpatrick of Stilwell, Oklahoma. The Aztec incantations were collected in the early 1600s by Hernando Ruiz de Alarcón of Atenango del Rio, Mexico—a little later than the era of Sahagún and his Indian helpers.

Aztec literature also includes a book of riddles, the so-called what-is-its. They are told in this manner: "What is it—a blue bowl filled with popcorn? Answer: it's the sky with its stars." Here is another: "What is it—ten little flat stones that we carry with us wherever we go? Answer: our fingernails." And "What has a white head and wears green feathers on top? An onion." "What wears a tight blouse? A tomato." "What is it that says to itself, 'You go that way, I'll go this way, we'll meet on the other side?' Answer: a loincloth." And one more: "What is it—a scarlet macaw leads the way, a raven brings up the rear? Answer: a grass fire."

We come finally to the narratives, the traditional histories and creation stories, that are perhaps the most familiar element in Aztec literature. These are preserved in a variety of sources, mostly in Nahuatl, a few in Spanish or other European languages, translated from lost Nahuatl originals.

There is the story of how the earth was created from the body of a woman. Forests were made from her hair; grass and flowers from her skin; mountains from her shoulders; valleys from her nose.

Another story tells how human life was created five times, each time under a different sun. The sun we see in the sky today, therefore, is the fifth sun. A similar view of world history remains current in the southwestern United States, where many Indian people—as some of you are no doubt aware—speak of present conditions or modern times as "the fifth world."

Another of the Aztec stories tells how corn was discovered inside a mountain; this is a story that is still told in many parts of Mexico and Central America.

Of particular interest in Aztec narrative lore is the theme of the powerful child. Quetzalcoatl himself, according to some storytellers, was such a child. He had three evil brothers, who hated him because he was his father's favorite. In a rage they murdered the father. To punish them, Quetzalcoatl put the three brothers to death, then went on to become the priest-king of Tula, the magnificent city to the north that rose and fell before the time of the Aztec empire.

The famous king Nezahualcoyotl of Texcoco, a city a few miles west of the Aztec capital, was also a powerful child. At the time of his birth the entire Valley of Mexico was terrorized by the cruel king Tezozomoc of the Tepanecs. One day, while the little boy Nezahualcoyotl was playing beside the water, he slipped and fell in. While underwater, he had a vision in which sorcerers spoke to him, saying, "You shall be the one. We ordain your fate, and by your hand a nation shall be destroyed." Then the boy went to the palace of King Tezozomoc and taunted him. Later he led an army that liberated the Valley.

Another of these children was the Aztec tribal deity, Huitzilopochtli, who came from his mother's womb wearing a full suit of armor and carrying weapons. It was he who led the wandering Aztecs from their ancestral homeland in the north, Aztlan, to the site of their future capital, Mexico City.

The figure of the terrifying or powerful child is by no means limited to Aztec lore. Examples can be found in many different Indian traditions. Among the Arapaho, for instance, we find the story of Raw Gums, who was born with a full set of teeth—a terrible little boy who crawled from lodge to lodge, eating up the neighbors. In the end, however, Raw Gums saved his people from the spirit of winter.[7] We recall that Quetzalcoatl, Nezahualcoyotl, and Huitzilopochtli were also saviors or leaders of their people.

The Nahuatl literary industry of sixteenth- and early-seventeenth-century Mexico not only put Aztec lore into permanent form but reached out to Old World lore and produced translations. The lives of the saints, including the life of St. Francis of Assisi, were put into Nahuatl; also the life of Christ, including the Nativity and the story of the Three Kings. "Adaptations" would be a better word than "translations," because when these familiar texts are translated *back* into a modern language, they carry with them the flavor of Aztec speech and Aztec customs. Aesop's *Fables,* sometimes referred to as the oldest work of children's literature, is another of the European classics that survives in a sixteenth-century Nahuatl version.

Finally, mention should be made of the Nahuatl text known as *Nican mopohua,* a phrase that simply means "here it is told"—in this case the legend of the poor man Juan Diego and the Virgin of Guadalupe, long regarded as an ideal story for children, not only in Mexico but in the United States.

In reviewing the available material, one is struck by the opportunities. Aztec literature study is a relatively new field. There are important Nahuatl manuscripts that have been translated only roughly and dozens of other manuscripts that have not yet been translated at all. Generally, if there is material of this sort that is of interest to children, they will have to wait while it is pored over and sifted by adult scholars; and gradually it trickles down. Why not give it first to children and let it trickle up? The pleasure of discovery can be as meaningful to children as it is to adults, even if it has to be taken on faith. To put the matter differently, people who speak English enjoy the discovery of a new poem by Shakespeare, whether or not they've read Shakespeare's other poems, the ones that have been in print for four hundred years.

The bringing to light of a text that has been buried for several centuries carries with it a special responsibility. Though it may seem to, on account of its antiquity, the text does not exist in a vacuum. It represents a people, whose remains may have ties to the present. The modern

Pueblo poet Simon J. Ortiz has written of finding in a museum display case the bones of a little girl, excavated from a pre-Pueblo archaeological site; he writes:

> Girl, my daughter, my mother,
> softly asleep.
> They have unearthed you.[8]

The lines are remarkable for their lack of reproach. But they do reveal the feelings that the ancestral cultures can arouse today for a Native American.

As I mentioned earlier, Aztec culture is one of those that continue to operate in people's minds. How should its literature be presented for readers today? If I say that authenticity, truthfulness, should be the guiding principle, I am sure that no one will disagree. Nevertheless, there is a persistent notion that truthfulness can be arrived at by the circuitous route of retelling, that a strange-sounding text can fulfill its destiny in the hands of a literary reshaper.

In the Americas we are fortunate to have traditional, oral literature that comes to us direct from its creators. This is not the case with the Greek myths, the fairy tales of Perrault, or even the *Kinder- und Hausmärchen* so meritoriously retold by the Brothers Grimm. Stories retold, or poems recast, from the American traditions can be meritorious, too. And in the process there can even be an element of revitalization. Let us enjoy retellings—while seeing them clearly for what they are, new creations. Let us also enjoy the originals in all their freshness, translated without addition or embellishment, and let us share them with children.

We come, then, to the twin questions, What will English-speaking children be interested in? and How much of it are we willing to let them hear? To some extent these questions are preposterous, or at least irrelevant, outside the modern European tradition, which has tried so hard over the past two or three hundred years to stake out a domain called children's literature. It has even been said that the very concept of childhood is an invention of post-Renaissance Europe. Formerly, and in many non-Western cultures, children were and are little adults, with prerogatives and sometimes harsh responsibilities, in a context generally free of sentimentalization. This point—in one of its aspects—was well made by the late Clyde Kluckhohn and Dorothea Leighton in their standard description of Navajo culture, from which I quote: "Rights of individuals, including children, . . . are respected to the fullest degree, even when their wishes run counter to the obvious interests of the family or extended family. [Tourists] seeking to purchase a bow and arrow that they see in a hogan are surprised to have adults refer the question to the five-year-old who owns the toy and whose decision is final."[9]

In my thumbnail sketch of Aztec childhood I have attempted to show the extent to which children, even newborns, participated in adult activities; and my brief description of Aztec literature is intended not to show what had been preselected for children—there is no evidence that anything in particular was withheld from them—but rather to indicate those elements they could have responded to on their own terms, keeping in mind what may be called the politics of childhood. In this gentle give and take, so often played out in literature—in impertinent riddles or in stories of magically powerful children—the child's weapons are levity, irreverence, mentioning the unmentionable, and the delicious violence that entails wicked kings, beheaded giants, and incinerated witches. In European culture, as in perhaps all cultures, adults make attempts to keep the situation under control. But children have subtle ways of protecting their interests. As a little boy in my neighborhood, a firm devotee of "Hansel and Gretel," reassured his grandmother not long ago, "The witch doesn't really die—because, when you read it again, she's there."

Clearly there are universal themes that bridge the gaps between literatures and between cultures. If it were otherwise, we would remain isolated within our familiar routines, unable to expand or reach out. The mystery and humor of genuine literature, from whatever culture, makes it easier to grasp the points of contact. By its very art, the translated song or the translated story can sweep us along. But underneath, a serious transaction is taking place, because each particular literature, each particular culture, is an ambassador for all the others. The child who is introduced to stories from the Aztec or the Navajo or the Japanese is taking out the scales and weighing the human race; and this is an opportunity that, for each child, can be repeated only a limited number of times.

How well are we doing? Looking back over the past hundred years of translated literature for children, we can see grievous errors in taste and errors in sensitivity. Yet it is a sign of progress that we can see this so plainly. I like to think that we are doing much better today. Perhaps in the near future we will do even better. This is the hope of every writer, and every translator. The next book will be better; we are always making a fresh beginning.

References

1. John Bierhorst, ed., *The Sacred Path* (New York: Morrow, 1983), p.18.
2. Ibid., p.25.
3. Ibid., p.26.
4. John Bierhorst, trans., *Cantares Mexicanos: Songs of the Aztecs* (Stanford, Calif.: Stanford Univ. Pr., 1985), p.269–71.
5. Bierhorst, *The Sacred Path,* p.48.
6. Jack Frederick Kilpatrick and Anna Gritts Kilpatrick, *Walk in Your Soul: Love Incantations of the Oklahoma Cherokees* (Dallas: Southern Methodist Univ. Pr., 1965), p.86–87; reprinted in Bierhorst, *The Sacred Path,* p.35.
7. George A. Dorsey and Alfred L. Kroeber, *Traditions of the Arapaho* (Chicago: Field Columbian Museum, 1903), p.231–36; reprinted in Bierhorst, *The Red Swan* (New York: Farrar, 1976), p.141–48.
8. Simon J. Ortiz, *A Good Journey* (Tucson: Univ. of Arizona Pr., 1977), p.108.
9. Clyde Kluckhohn and Dorothea Leighton, *The Navaho,* rev. ed. (Garden City, N.Y.: Doubleday/Anchor, 1962), p.310.

Bibliography

On Aztec childhood and education:

Durán, Diego de. *Historia de la Indias de Nueva España e islas de la tierra firme.* Ed. by Angel

M. Garibay. V.1, *Libro de los ritos y ceremonies . . .* and *El calendario antiguo.* Mexico: Porrúa, 1967. Especially p.47–59.

Motolinía [Fray Toribio de Benavente]. *Memoriales o libro de las cosas de la Nueva España y de los naturales de ella.* Ed. by Edmundo O'Gorman. Mexico: Universidad Nacional Autónoma de México, 1971. Especially p.75, 308-9, 384, 439.

Ross, Kurt, ed. *Codex Mendoza: Aztec Manuscript.* N.p.: Miller Graphics, 1978(?). Especially p.69–95.

Sahagún, Bernardino de. *Florentine Codex: General History of the Things of New Spain.* Ed. by Arthur J. O. Anderson and Charles E. Dibble. Parts 1–13 (Introductory volume and books 1–12). Santa Fe, N.M.: School of American Research and Univ. of Utah Pr., 1st ed., 1950–82; 2d ed., rev. (book 1), 1970. Especially book 1 (2d ed.), p.50, 82; book 2, p.120, 156–57, 181; book 3, p.64; book 4, p.3–4, 34, 73, 114; book 5, p.195; book 6, p.167, 227; book 8, p.71–72; book 9, p.88, 95; book 10, p.2–3, 89.

Sources of Aztec literature:

Alarcón, Hernando Ruiz de. *Treatise on the Heathen Superstitions.* Trans. and ed. by J. Richard Andrews and Ross Hassig. Norman: Univ. of Oklahoma Pr., 1984. Incantations.

Bierhorst, John, trans. *Cantares Mexicanos: Songs of the Aztecs.* Stanford, Calif.: Stanford Univ. Pr., 1985. Poetry.

________. *Codex Chimalpopoca.* Forthcoming. Stories.

Kutscher, Gerdt, Gordon Brotherston, and Günter Vollmer. *Aesop in Mexico.* Berlin: Gebr. Mann, 1987. Fables.

Sahagún, Bernardino de. *Florentine Codex* (see above). Stories (books 3 and 7), ritual orations (book 6), riddles (book 6).

________. *Psalmodia christiana, y sermonario de los sanctos del año, en lengua mexicana.* Mexico: Pedro Ocharte, 1583. Saints' lives, life of Christ.

Velázquez, Primo Feliciano. *Huei tlamahuiçoltica . . . : libro en lengua mexicana que el Br. Luis Lasso de la Vega hizo imprimir en México el año de 1649.* Mexico: Carreño & hijo, 1926. Legend of the Virgin of Guadalupe.

Margaret Mahy

A Dissolving Ghost

POSSIBLE OPERATIONS OF TRUTH IN CHILDREN'S BOOKS AND THE LIVES OF CHILDREN

Margaret Mahy

is a New Zealand author of over forty books for a wide range of ages from preschool through adolescence. Her writing is generally characterized by its clarity of language, rich humor and exuberance, spectacular invention and control, and keen understanding of human relationships. Ms. Mahy received the New Zealand Library Association's Esther Glen Medal for *Lion in the Meadow* (U.S. edition: Franklin Watts, 1969); *The First Margaret Mahy Storybook* (Dent, 1972); *The Haunting* (U.S. edition: Atheneum, 1982); and *The Changeover; A Supernatural Romance* (U.S. edition: Atheneum, 1984). The Library Association of England's Carnegie Medal was awarded to *The Haunting* and *The Changeover. The Boy Who Was Followed Home* (U.S. edition: Franklin Watts, 1975) and *The Changeover* are ALA Notables. Before becoming a full-time writer, Ms. Mahy was a school librarian and a children's librarian in Christchurch, New Zealand. She lives in Governors Bay in the South Island of New Zealand.

FIRST OF ALL I want to thank you for the invitation to give this lecture. As a librarian I have been reading other Arbuthnot lectures for years and years and from time to time I have felt like Tove Jansson's Moomintroll watching the sea horses dance. You may remember that Moomintroll suddenly thinks he is beautiful, (mistakenly as it happens) and longs to join in the dance. On this occasion I have been invited to be a temporary dancer. Thank you very much.

The Lovers and the Shark

Two years ago it happened I found myself in a motel swimming pool in New Mexico. I like swimming. I swim quite purposefully and I had the swimming pool almost to myself—not quite, however. At the shallow end of the pool stood a young man and woman passionately, indeed it sometimes seemed permanently, embraced. I didn't mind this while I was swimming away from them, but as I swam towards them I found myself filled with the embarrassment of someone who is intruding into a private space, a space which one has no right to violate. My shyness, my wish not to intrude upon this couple, alternated with something less charitable, self-righteous indignation. After all this was not a private space; it was a motel swimming pool and I was swimming backwards and forwards, which everyone knows is the proper thing to do in a swimming pool. Why should I be the one to feel intrusive and guilty? I felt like this swimming away from them. Then swimming towards them I began to think—ah, but am I jealous of their youth and passion and so on, (kicking regularly, surging to the other end of the pool). Yet who wants to be bothered with self-analysis when you are trying to shoot through the water like a silver arrow? As I swam backwards and forwards I began to dream of dressing up as a shark, and gliding, up the pool towards them. I could see myself soundless, menacing, and ruthless, my skin set with sharp close-set menacing and ruthless, my skin set with sharp close-set denticles, my silent crescent snarl filled with rows and rows of teeth. The lovers would suddenly see my dorsal fin approaching. They would leap out of the water screaming. I would have the whole pool to myself, free to be a silver arrow to my heart's content. It would all be *my* space, and deservedly so.

After I left the pool, I found myself haunted, not by the lovers themselves but by the one who had wanted all the space in the swimming pool. This person usurping the primitive power of the shark, the fin cutting through the water, the huge mouthful of teeth rising up over the back of the boat—this temporary villain I had contemplated becoming, in order to have all the swimming pool to myself. It had in some ways been a tempting and empowering persona, and one I recognised, although I

Presented April 23, 1989, at the William Pitt Student Union, University of Pittsburgh. The 1989 Arbuthnot Lecture is sponsored by Scott, Foresman and Company in cooperation with the Association for Library Service to Children, the American Library Association, Children's Services at The Carnegie Library (Pittsburgh), and the School of Library and Information Science at the University of Pittsburgh.

had never met it in that shape before. My temporary shark began to make other sharkish connections. Sharks have been part of my life for a long time. Though shark attacks are almost unknown in New Zealand, we all know the sharks are there. Parents sometimes warn their children, "Don't go out deep! There might be sharks!" Of course the children already know. Sharks!

Once, dramatically, I saw a shark caught on a hand line pulled up and left to die on the sand. It was only a small one, but it was a genuine shark. I stood over it watching it drown in the sunny air of a remote North Island beach. When it began to rot away, someone threw it back into the deep water where smaller fish flickered around it for a while eating what was left, but even then its bones still glimmered mysteriously through the water if you knew where to look. It was the year I turned five. It was also the year I learned to swim. I couldn't write much in those days, but was already a slave to fiction. I talked aloud, waving sticks in the air, conducting unseen orchestras of stories remembered, recreated and invented, stories which I inhabited by temporarily becoming what I was inventing. That shark and the mystery and menace of the glimmering bones and what might have happened (that it might have been *my* bones glimmering there, I suppose) were part of those stories in those days. It was certainly part of the first nightmare I can ever remember having: that my little sister vanished under the water and after a second or two her sunbonnet came floating to the top. We were living in a caravan in those days. I woke up in the top bunk crying, and bewildered to find that something which only a moment before had seemed utterly real had dissolved into nothing. I think it was the same shark, flesh on its bones once more, that came out of the past to inhabit me and swim up and down the motel swimming pool. It's just as well I didn't have my shark suit with me.

I like to swim in deep water. I like to be where I can't feel the bottom and I have always liked that from the time I was very small, but there is always the fear of the shark sneaking up from down below grabbing your foot. After you've been frightened of it for a while, you begin to tell stories about it, to take it over . . . and in odd moments of life when you have a little go at being the shark yourself, you recognise something true in what you are doing.

A Marvellous Code

I am going to propose that there is a code in our lives, something we automatically recognise when we encounter it in the outside world, something personal, but possibly primeval, too, something which gives form to our political responses, to our art, our religious feelings sometimes to our science and, recently in New Zealand at least, to the way the weather forecast is presented as little drama. It is something eagerly recognised by young children, so perhaps there is no first encounter. Perhaps it is already in them. My own experience of it has been that, by giving experience a recognisable structure, it has also made it easier to recall and use. It makes use of cause and effect, though sometimes it precedes and transcends it. It can be suspected or duplicated but I don't think it can be really dismantled. Broken to bits, it starts to reassemble itself like the Iron Man described by Ted Hughes, and creeps back into our lives patient but inexorable.

A Misleading Question

Many years ago now, I read for the first time a novel by Noel Streatfeild called *Ballet Shoes,* possibly the book for which she is best known. Most of you will know that it is the story of three children: Pauline, Petrova, and Posy Fossil who took this surname because they were all adopted by a kindly fossil hunter, Great Uncle Matthew or GUM. It tells of their lives at home and on the stage, and is a career and a family story in the one book. Some years later, in the act of being a librarian, I found in a library stack an adult novel by Noel Streatfeild, written in 1931, five years before *Ballet Shoes* was published. It was called *The Whicharts* and was about a family of three girls and their lives at home and on the stage, and it tells the same story as *Ballet Shoes,* but tells it for adults. The three girls are now revealed as half-sisters, all illegitimate daughters of a charming but irresponsible, well-born Englishman. They are cared for by a woman (the Sylvia of *Ballet Shoes*) who loved him deeply in spite of his facile character and who grew to love his daughters as if they were her own. He dies leaving them in difficult circumstances and in an effort to make a reasonable middle-class living, the girls become involved in life on the wicked stage. The story pursues them through adolescence, tells us how the girl who corresponds to Pauline in *Ballet Shoes* is seduced, I think by a theatrical director, and how the one who corresponds to Petrova actually locates her mother after their loving guardian dies, and finds herself shyly welcomed by a woman as odd and adventurous as she is herself. The family in this book is not called the Fossils, but the Whicharts (a name which also involves a play on words, however, coming as it does from their mishearing of something in the Lord's prayer, *Our Father, which art in heaven,* something eloquent to children who had been told, on debatable evidence I must say, that that's where their father was). I was fascinated by all this new information which suggested that Noel Streatfeild certainly knew more about the family than she had revealed in *Ballet Shoes* and I gave the book to a friend of mine who had enjoyed *Ballet Shoes.* She read it and, feeling betrayed in some intangible way, became very angry. "It just made me wonder—how much truth should we tell children?" she said, asking a leading question which is also misleading.

Well, it is an old debate with many answers. For instance I don't think Noel Streatfeild would have been allowed to tell everything she knew about the Fossils in a children's book back in 1936, though she certainly would be permitted to tell more today, since our interpretation of childhood has altered since then. As an adult reading *Ballet Shoes* I am now always aware of that ghostly *other* story, that extra truth, and something about the nature of my adult experience makes me think that *The Whicharts* is the truer story partly because that was the way it was told first, but also because, as an adult, I see a stronger rationale in the adult story. I think *Ballet Shoes* is a better book for what it is than *The Whicharts* for what *it* is, and yet, for all that, I feel I have unfair knowledge, for I can't help including what I know of the adult story as part of the truth of *Ballet Shoes.* I say to myself "This is what was really happening, but we couldn't tell the kids." Unlike my friend I don't think Noel Streatfeild should have either insisted on telling the full truth or not told any of it. No one tells the full truth anyway and children's literature would have been the poorer for not having *Ballet Shoes.* Nevertheless I have never forgotten my friend's question, and there is a dislocation in my feelings about it all—a sort of puzzlement which I am perhaps unfairly trying to get rid of by passing it on to others.

How much truth do we tell children? We certainly encourage them to tell all the truth themselves. I impressed on my children what my mother had impressed on me, that we should always tell the truth. (Funnily enough, now that they're grown-up I quite often find that I wish they wouldn't and I know my mother often wished I would shut up.) How much truth we choose to tell children is an important question, but not a fair one. How much truth should we tell grown-ups for that matter? After all children often want to know about things and adults often don't. A lot of people want to protect the innocence of childhood but isn't it also a pity to disturb security and innocence in adulthood? Sometimes we just don't like to see people living happy lives for what we perceive as wrong reasons. This poor single word "truth" has to bear a heavy burden. It's not fair to ask one word to do so much, and unlike Humpty Dumpty, we exploit our labour force. We don't pay words extra when we ask them to do a lot of work for us.

Fact and Fiction

I was born in 1936, the year *Ballet Shoes* was published, and from the time I was very small I was encouraged to listen to stories. I began as a listener, and then, since I wanted to join in that particular dance, I put together stories of my own, as I have already mentioned, telling them aloud to walls and trees. Because I couldn't write back then, I learned them by heart as a way of containing them, but I went on to become a reader, and very shortly after that learned to write and began to contain them by putting them down in notebooks. I began as a listener, became a teller, then a reader, and then a writer in that order. Later still I became a librarian, which in some ways is the ultimate result of this evolutionary process, since a lot of library work is concerned with orderly containment. (But I must advise you to beware a little of my description of myself which is automatically starting to gather the elements of a romantic story around itself.)

Being a librarian forces you to think a lot about truth and to pretend you have gotten over any confusions you might ever had over it. You have a book, it has to go in some particular physical place in the library shelves. It can't really be both here and there. Even if you have a big enough book grant and can afford to buy two copies of the same book and put it in two different places, a book like *The Endless Steppe,* say, is not quite the same story in the nonfiction shelves that it is in the fiction (where it was rather more likely to be read in our library at least.) If you are a librarian (allowing for the general advice we get about putting a book where it is going to be looked for and best used) you have fiction on one side of the library and nonfiction on the other. Ask a child the difference between fiction and nonfiction and the child will often answer nonfiction is true and fiction is not true. "That's right," we say. "Fiction is not true and nonfiction is." But writers and readers often dispute this simple division, and I'm sure there must be many librarians like me—librarians who suddenly find themselves staring around wildly at their library walls (all that *knowledge,* all that *emotion,* all that *astonishment!* What am I doing here at the intersecting focus of all these great fields? I am trying to *shelve* it!) their own sense of reality terminally eroded by service for others. Making books available in the most sensible way makes us aware that in serving one function we are distorting others. We are standing astride the line of a great dislocation.

Dislocations in a True Landscape

I am used to dislocations. I have more than one running right through me. Dislocation is in some ways an image of the country I grew up in, and it has to be one image of the U.S.A. I think, even we agree to call it diversity. If dislocation wasn't the *source* of my sense of things not matching up, of them rushing together and immediately beginning to fall apart, it is to some extent the mirror of them.

New Zealand, the country which is in every meaningful way my home, is a country in the Pacific Ocean, but my family was European not Polynesian, and consciously and unconsciously regarded the European, and more specifically British, culture as the highest form of civilization in the world. The result was a big imaginative displacement, for, though there were a few children's books written in and about New Zealand when I was a child, the majority of stories including those that inexorably fixed me, came largely from Britain with a few, a very few, from the U.S.A. Coming in from swimming on Christmas Day I would sit with my sun hat on, reading stories of snow and robins and holly and though I have never once spent a Christmas in the Northern hemisphere, those things are now part of my Christmas nostalgia. The imaginative truth and the factual truth are at odds with one another but I still need those opposites to make Christmas come alive for me . . . the sunny sea and the awareness of dark firs on snowy hillsides. But containing and synthesising such contradictions is easy for an imagination nourished on stories in which all becomes possible. I did indeed grow up with a fault line running through me, but that is a very New Zealandish feature when you consider that it is a country of earthquakes and volcanoes. A fault line ran right through the town I was born in so perhaps my disjunction is part of what makes an essential New Zealander of me after all. Perhaps the country has imposed its own unstable geography on my power to perceive. I don't mind. I regret it only in the sense that one always regrets not being able to be everything all at once. Dislocations can expose the secret nature of the land. They can make for an intensely interesting landscape, provided one doesn't come to feel that a landscape full of fault lines is the only legitimate kind. Dislocations made me a world reader rather than a local one, and they made me contingent rather than categorical.

New Zealand at the present is celebrating in a small way the development of a more indiginous children's fiction than at any time previously. Having at last got a foothold in the imagination of its writers, New Zealand is now an innate part of most of its indigenous children's books, which are increasingly free of unnaturally deliberate reference, of the self-consciousness that marked the first attempts to have *I am a New Zealander Writing about New Zealand* as a sort of sub text. There is a certain relieved mood of congratulation within the writing community, and a lot of talk, some of it meretricious, I think, about "relevance".

I think it is most important that a local literature should exist, so that the imaginations of children are colonised in the first instance by images from their immediate world. I am not in favour of dislocation for the sake of dislocation. But I am curious, too, about why I should have become such an enthusiastic reader myself when so little of what was immediately relevant was offered to me, and why, on the rare occasions that I did encounter books presenting my own street and my own idiom, I tended to pass them over in favour of exotic alternatives. Why was it that what seemed truest to me had nothing to do with the facts and images of my everyday life, which, mistakenly enough, I came to regard as inadequate stuff for a story?

Truth and Desire

In his celebrated essay *Tree and Leaf,* Tolkein speculates about why Andrew Lang turned his adult study of myth and folklore into a series of stories for children. "*I suspect*" Lang apparently says, *"that belief and appetite for marvels are regarded as identical or closely related. They are radically different, though the appetite for marvels is not at once or at first differentiated by a growing human mind from its general appetite.*" Lang, according to Tolkein, may be implying that the teller of marvellous tales to children trades on the credulity that makes it less easy for children to distinguish fact from fiction "*though,*" (Tolkein says, correctly I think,) "*the distinction is fundamental to the human mind, and to fairy stories.*" All the same I think that the appetite for marvels may reinforce some aspects of truth that the fact or fiction dichotomy seems to obscure.

Talking further about the appetite for marvels, and his own appetite for reading, Tolkein then says of himself,

> I had no special wish to believe. . . . At no time can I remember that the enjoyment of a story was dependent on belief that such things could happen or had happened in real life. Fairy stories were plainly not concerned with possibility but with desirability. If they awakened desire, satisfying it while whetting it unbearably, they succeeded.

I think that, like Tolkein and many readers before and since, I was filled with an appetite for marvels, and desire alone seemed to me to be a sufficient justification for a story, even though longing for what is not true has been seen as a wicked thing to do, particularly by those readers who also strenuously maintain that we should not disturb the innocence of children by telling them all the truth. I tend to think, since the appetite for marvels appears to be so much a part of humanity, that it exists in us for a reason, and that in an odd way it is connected with truth. My enjoyment of a story did not depend on belief while I was reading the story, for the story generated its own belief, but afterwards I would often try to adjust the world so that the story could be fitted into it. To find something that was marvellous was wonderful, to find something that was both wonderful and true was ecstacy, for it meant wonderful things might be possible for me, too.

"*The function of the storyteller is to relate the truth in a manner that is simple, to integrate without reduction, for it is barely possible to declare the truth as it is, because the universe presents itself as a mystery. We have to find parables; we have to tell stories to unriddle the world,*" explains Alan Garner going on to say that the story is a symbol. Since all the important processes of our lives (like eating and reproducing) are reinforced with powerful pleasure principles, perhaps we are constructed to look for pleasure in stories, to desire them, because we need to know about them and to be able to use them. Stories enable us first to give form to, and then to take possession of, a variety of truths both literal and figurative. Once we have part of truth caught up in a story we can name it and get some sort of power over it. But, of course, we have to be careful about the way we believe stories. They can make us not only into temporary heroes and wizards, but also temporary villains, too . . . even into sharks.

Poor Judgements

When I was a small child and read *King Solomon's Mines,* a book inherited from my father, I knew it was an invention. And when I read in another of my father's childhood books (Volume One of an Edwardian edition of *Arthur Mee's Encyclopaedia*), that the Earth had once been a fiery ball and that it had dropped off the Sun, I knew it was true. The encyclopaedia was true and *King Solomon's Mines* wasn't. Nevertheless at one stage I tried to tell a cousin of mine that the events in *King Solomon's Mines* were historical facts even though I knew they weren't, trying by powerful assertion, by faith alone, to drag the story through to sit alongside by the fiery ball which had fallen off the Sun. Well, it wouldn't go. I needed an identical act of faith from other people to give it even the semblence of this other truth, and no one else would agree to play that game with me. I was alone with the story and my desire for it to be true. It wasn't the only attempt I made to bring a marvellous fiction through into the real world, to force a general agreement that I was in charge of truth and not the other way around. From the time I was seven until I was about ten I publicly maintained and defended the proposition that I could talk the language of the animals. The immediate source of this assertion was *The Jungle Book* (not the book but a film of the book, the one starring Sabu and a variety of real animals). My mother must have enjoyed it, too, because, for the only time in my childhood that I can remember I was taken to see a film twice. I couldn't bear that that particular story should remain in what I then perceived as the half-life of fiction. Coleridge has described works of fiction as acts of secondary creation and I wanted to make *The Jungle Book* primary. I wanted to make it as if it had been created by God and not by man.

In order to achieve this I publicly claimed and tried to demonstrate that I had the powers of Mowgli. Challenged, I would talk an invented gibberish that fooled nobody, least of all any passing dogs or birds, and not one of the lively knowing children around me. So I became more and more extreme in my attempts to demonstrate my oneness with animal creation. I ate leaves in public, all sorts of leaves, children came up to me in the playground and offered me leaves which I ate indiscriminately. I drank from roadside puddles as dogs do. Of course I was subjected to derision which I deserved for poor judgement if nothing else. I knew all the time I couldn't really speak the language of the animals in the world of primary creation, but I imagine now I wanted people to come into the secondary world with me, a world in which I had given myself a starring role. I do believe there were elements of the story existing in me already, that it was not that Kipling's imagination, filtered through the medium of the film, imposed itself on me, but that something already in me leaped out to make a powerful connection. Certainly at some levels I was powerless to resist whatever it was that came crashing in or perhaps out. Nor I am suggesting that this susceptibility is a thing to be uncritically encouraged. I do think, however, that it is far from unique and in order for it to be understood it needs to be described. It certainly can be dangerous (after all I could have poisoned myself eating vegetation that unqualified way) but the same thing can be said of a lot of human reactions including patriotism and love and even truth itself; they're all very risky. Anyhow, having received that story, I think I had to incorporate it, having incorporated it I had to discharge it, and, as I was young and simple the discharging took a wrong turn, an inappropriately literal one.

Now oddly enough, at the same time that I was being teased about my claim to talk the language of the animals, I was subject to an equal derision, which once resulted in my being chased home by indignant children, some of them cousins of mine which seemed to add insult to injury. I publicly asserted that the Earth had once dropped off the Sun, that I had a picture at home that proved it, and added on the same authority (that of *Arthur Mee's Encyclopaedia*) that the world would some day, a million years from now, come to an end. I can remember running home with other outraged children after me, turning in at a strange gate, knocking on a door and saying to the astonished woman who answered it that children were waiting outside to beat me up because I said the world had once fallen off the Sun and that it would come to an end one day. I was confident that an adult would recognise and confirm the truth I was telling and rally to support it.

Well, whether she believed it or not, there was nothing she could do to help me. Of course, if you present certain facts too confidently it sounds as if you are taking personal credit for them, and perhaps I sounded as if I was the one who had caused the world to fall off the Sun in the first place and would one day will its end. And I certainly don't want to sound as if I'm standing here in Pittsburgh winging it, because I didn't have the respect I should have had at school. I think I deserved all I got for eating leaves and drinking from puddles, which is not a sign of superior sensibility only of poor judgement, tragically coupled with the will to be marvellous. I totally agree with the person who said that a difficult time at school doesn't necessarily entitle you to write a novel. But what I do want to record is that nonfiction could provoke as much derision, disbelief and resentment as fantasy and just to make the situation a little more complicated, nowadays, no astronomer seems to believe that the Earth ever fell off the Sun. The other children were right to suspect it, even if they suspected it for the wrong reasons. What I learned as truth back then was another mistake.

Variations on a Divine Gift

Because of the way science has developed over the last 300 years, we do live in a time when we expect truth to be objectively provable. Measurement is a vital part of our lives today. We live, our children along with us, in a very mathematised society. In the past, before Tycho Brahe, if a minor detail did not fit into a major hypothesis it was easy to shrug it away. The idea that anyone might be accountable to that sort of truth was a foreign one. But Kepler, in computing the orbit of Mars, acknowledged as significant an error of eight minutes of arc which Copernicus had been able to ignore. Kepler wrote "*But for us, who by divine kindness, were given an accurate observer such as Tycho Brahe, for us it is fitting we should acknowledge this divine gift and put it to use*" and what Whitehead describes as "stubborn and irreducible fact" became increasingly important. Like Kepler I believe intricate and accurate measurement is a gift we are given by divine kindness, and that the inventive mind, coming up against stubborn and irreducible facts, has to capitulate and look for richness and amazement within that capitulation. Today "stubborn and irreducible facts" seem paramount because of the kind of power that attention to such details confers, including the power to make money which often involves the power to get one's own way, very seductive powers indeed. So "stubborn and irreducible facts" are frequently seen as coinciding with truth, or truth is seen as being the same sort of thing as the facts are and nothing more. It often seems to me that deterministic accounts of existence never quite face up to the fact that they don't eliminate mystery but merely shift it into areas where it can be acceptably labeled. And history shows all sort of abberations built even into part of the truth we shelve in the 500s.

For example, in the beginning of chapter sixteen of his book *New Astronomy* Kepler, who thought of accurate observation as a divine gift, absentmindedly put three erroneous figures for three vital longitudes of Mars and then towards the end of the chapter committed several mistakes in simple arithmetic which virtually cancelled his first mistakes out so that he got more or less the right answer. At the most crucial point in the process of discovering his Second Law Kepler again made a series of mathematical errors that cancelled themselves out allowing him to arrive at a correct result. What sort of truth was operating there? Perhaps something was so determined to be discovered that even mathematical error was forced to yield a true result? Somewhere recently I read that

Mendel cheated in recording the results of his experiments on genetic inheritance in peas and produced a nice pattern that illuminated what currently passes for truth and is taught in 6th form biology in New Zealand schools. Perhaps something wants to be found. Nowadays we are told that even chaos has a structure.

Earlier in this century, 1903 to be precise, at the time when much thrilling new information on radiation was coming to hand, René Blondlot, an experienced physicist, discovered a new ray which he called an N ray, one of the characteristics of which was that it treated substances opaque to visible light, including wood, iron silver, etc., as if they were transparent. Many notable scientists, particularly French ones, subsequently detected the same ray. But the American physicist R. W. Wood found he was absolutely unable to reproduce Blondlot's striking results. Blondlot and his colleagues later declared that it was the sensitivity of the observer not the validity of the phenomena that was in question, but by 1905 only French scientists, and by no means all of them, believed in the N ray (though some of them still maintained that only the Latin races had sufficient sensitivity to detect the N ray, that fog had ruined the perception of Anglo-Saxon observers and beer the perception of the German ones). Nowadays no one believes the N ray ever existed. The *Scientific American* (May 1980) from which I got much of this good information says that the times had psychologically prepared Blondlot to discover a new sort of radiation.

I suggest that one might say with equal truth that he was imaginatively prepared to eat leaves and drink from puddles, but the way in which he did this matched up so closely with accepted reality and with desire that he did what I could not do, he actually altered perception for a while and won people to his side. Scientific truths, which should be pure and objective, can stagger and sway on their way to becoming recognised as scientific truths, can be as bizarre as the plots of the stories they partly resemble, or the stories that are told about them afterwards. Yet, though the scientists who advised the editors of *Arthur Mee's Encyclopaedia* about the beginning of the world had made what I now take to be a genuine mistake, it was a mistake that fixed my attention in childhood, and (it is even tempting to think) enabled me to see something true which stayed true, even when the information turned out to be false. If so, the true thing was wonder . . . wonder which dissolves into Tolkein's desire, and so I have come to think wonder must be a part of truth, but a part which our physical systems are anxious to conceal. A perpetual state of wonder and desire (which seems to me the truest state to be in, confronted with the universe) is certainly not the most practical state to try and live in. We are biologically engineered to have the wonder filtered out of our lives, to learn to take astonishing things for granted so that we don't waste too much energy on being surprised but get on with the eating and mating, gardening, feeding cats, complaining about taxes, and so on. We have the power to entertain visions, but operate best when most things are humdrum. When I first flew in an areoplane it was an experience of amazement. Now I think of the flying time (a time when gravity is confounded, when a metal machine filled with people rises more or less safely into the air) as time when I am going to get a chance to read without any guilty feeling that I should be doing something else. To encounter the amazements, partly compounded of fear and beauty, which I recognised so eagerly when I was a child I now have given myself the space to achieve a rare and difficult mood, or to search through new disclosures of science and history, or, more frequently, to read a story.

I've certainly never had any trouble abandoning the falling-off-the-Sun theory in favour of the Big Bang and slow condensation out of the stuff of the primordial universe. I know by now the facts, even marvellous ones, slide around, and that people get things wrong, and the truest thing in science is wonder just as it is in story. And I never forget that the story is as important to human beings as science, more powerful at times because it is more subversive.

A Fairy Tale Disguised

If any story I have told has the mark of social realism on it, it is certainly *Memory,* and in it I have told young readers a lot of the truth I know about the metamorphosis of a rational human being replete with knowledge, memory and the power to make a cup of tea several times a day, into a demented old woman losing command of all the things in which self-respect is traditionally established, and driven to wear a tea cosy instead of a hat.

For a number of years I was in charge of my aunt, and though my aunt and Sophie are not the same person, they are similar in many ways. A lot of the happenings, a lot of the conversations, in *Memory* are directly transposed from my life with my aunt, and if the story lacks the nastiness, the sheer fatigue of response involved in looking after a demented person, it is partly because, though those elements were present, they were not a commanding part of my life with aunt. Because I had a background of story to draw on she never lost her imaginative function in my life. An English review criticised the book because, somehow, at the end, Sophie was tidied up rather too quickly, but there are two odd things about that. One is that in the real world once I indicated I needed help I actually got a certain amount. The support services were good, partly because I was sufficiently well-educated to know where to go and what sort of things to say, and also because I was prepared to cope with quite a lot before I asked for some support. A district nurse and a housekeeper appeared, once a week and things were tidied up quite quickly. In between times things went downhill, but neither my aunt or I bothered too much about a certain amount of squalor.

The other odd thing is that because *Memory* is full of factual experiences which are readily recognisable, and because it deals with an area that, in New Zealand at least, enjoys a reasonably high public profile at present, it may seem to be intended as a book of social realism. However for me it is fairy tale of a sort. The fantasy of earlier books of mine is still present, but in the imaginative sub text rather than explicit in any happenings in the story because that fantasy is part of truth of my own life and I cannot truthfully omit it. I didn't set out to write a fairy tale but, in an effort to convey truthfully the quality of the experiences I had had, I found myself telling the story of a young man who, having quarrelled with his father, set out into the world with no blessing and no money to make his fortune. He meets a strange old woman needing help, a strange old woman who asks him a question, and through giving her the help she needs, he answers the question and is strengthened by the answer. His response to her determines the way he learns just as the kind responses of third sons or younger princes to the old people and animals they meet on their journeys results in them finding their fortunes. These elements are recognisably fairy tale elements I think.

Yet something like this fairy tale really happened in Christchurch once. A gang of rather derelict young people took over a house in which a demented old woman was living. Neighbours called in the social workers who found she was actually being looked after though admittedly in a rough and ready fashion. She was being fed regularly and bathed, talked to, and cared for. Her unlikely companions seemed to be fond of her, and after all there was no one else to look after her and nowhere for her to go, as all appropriate homes had waiting lists. I was told this story when I was already writing *Memory* by a social worker to whom I mentioned the book. And the first idea for the story came to me, as so many ideas do, as a haunting image seen from the window of a car in the early hours of the morning. Driving home though an empty city at about 2 a.m., I saw an old man coming out of a supermarket car park pushing an empty trolly. The image stayed with me until I found a place for it.

Now I am not trying to suggest my story is true because it contains its share of irreducible facts, or even particularly good because of them. I mention the facts and associated anecdotes because they are eloquent in their own way, but just as much of the truth of this story, always supposing it has any, lies in its form which seems to me to come from folktale, which has combined with many other things to give me a code by which to decipher experience. I used it in part to interpret my experiences with my aunt, so when I came to tell the truth, as it were, about those experiences I could not do so without conscious and unconscious references to folk tale. *Memory* has been described as tackling the subject of Alzheimer's disease, but it seems to me that it doesn't so much tackle it as recognise it, for the story is not in essence about Alzheimer's disease, but about a magical encounter between two unlikely people both of whom are possessed, in different ways by a dissolving rationality. It is intended to be a serious story composed of many different sorts of truth, yet if I was asked to give a quick answer to the question "Is it true?" I would have to say "No. It isn't true. All the same I have tried make it tell part of the truth."

And so at last by fading paths I come back to a different sort of story . . . to the shark who wanted all the swimming space to himself.

The Great White Maneating Shark

As I have already indicated the initial incident, true in the most literal sense of the word, began to hook itself into many others, some past, some present, some fantastic, some commonplace but all part of a personal reality. The imaginative process involved is not so much an instantaneous flash of inspiration as an act . . . a series of acts . . . of synthesis, the ideas and associations forming a network, rather than a linear account, a network in which the spaces between the cords are as important as the irreducible knots that hold the whole thing together.

Fantasy writers are not noted for their adherence to truth. In fact often their books are seen as being ways of deliberately escaping from what is true into what is not true. However, to quote Angela Carter, imagination, severed from reality festers, and writers of fantasy are often anxious to demonstrate that they are tied into real life in some way, and to claim that they have a part to play there too. We may claim to deal with abstract truths rather than mere facts, or perhaps that we deal in metaphor. But behind the printed page crouches the story, looking out at us between the lines that have temporarily caged it, making it stand still so that it can be considered. First stories were approximations to history and science, though nowadays science and story are seen as separate and maybe even antagonistic, science being an outer adventure while story is an inner one, if I may anticipate something Walter de la Mare said about story which I will quote later.

As I thought about my temporary sharkness, it suggested a simple story which I would find entertaining to write. There are a lot of different sorts of sharks, many of them quite harmless but I wanted to evoke the most sinister of all, the great white man-eating shark. I wanted there to be no misunderstanding about just what sort of shark this was. This reminded me of a piece in Russell Hoban's novel *Turtle Diary* which I promptly began to search for.

One of the narrators, Neaera, herself a writer for children, has read of an attempt by a rich man to photograph a great white shark. "*Eventually they found a great white shark which they attracted with whale oil, blood, and horsemeat. It was a truely terrifying creature and they very wisely stayed in their cage while the shark took the bars in his teeth and shook them about.*" She then goes on to say that socially the rich man was out of his class "*the shark would not have swum from ocean to ocean seeking them. It would have gone on its mute and deadly way, mindlessly being its awful self, innocent and murderous. It was the people who lusted for the attention of the shark.*"

Well, perhaps by reading and writing stories I too am guilty of trying to attract the attention of wonderful sharks. Locked in the cage of words I have stared out entranced while wonderful sharks took the bars of my cage in their teeth and shook it, and as I have already indicated I am capable to some extent at least of being a shark and worrying at the bars. Thinking of my own temporary sharkness I wrote a short story, entitled "The Great White Man Eating Shark."

Like most stories I write, I intended it primarily as a story to be told aloud, but it has been produced as a picture book, and tells the story of the villain, a plain boy who happens to be a very good actor and who dressed up as a great white man eating shark, frightening other swimmers out of the sea so that he could have it all to himself. He acted the part so well that a female shark fell in love with him and proposed something approximating marriage. He fled from her in terror. His duplicity was revealed, and he was too scared to go swimming for a long time after. This is obviously didactic (but, I hope ironically didactic), and seems far from true, since we all know that in real life firstly people do not dress up as sharks, and that the figurative sharks often go undetected because they don't allow people to see their dorsal fins. But in another way I have told the children all the truth I know from personal experience. Kurt Vonnegut says in the introduction to *Mother Night* "We are what we pretend to be, so we must be careful of what we pretend to be." That turned out to be the hidden truth of my New Mexico swimming pool experience, but would that have been its hidden truth if I hadn't already read books like *Mother Night*, or if I didn't already know in a personal way that we become what we pretend to be. I did not learn to talk the language of animals through eating leaves and drinking out of puddles, but I was chased and herded and treated rather like an animal for all that.

But the story of the shark is a joke and that is how I expect it to be enjoyed, as a joke and only as a joke. It is only in the context of this occasion that I am bothering to tell about the experience compacted in it, offering it as a joke at my own expense and also a part of a network, to a child who may one day read *Mother Night* or other books whose titles I can't guess at, and appreciate the truths in those books because they already know them. My own experience was real, funny, momentarily sinister and salutary, all at once, but someone else in that swimming pool on that day might have seen a different, a more anguished truth, might have realized that the lovers were saying goodbye, or that they were meeting after a long separation, or that they were honeymooners, or that the thought of being together without touching was unbearable to them. A thousand other stories were potentially there in the swimming pool with me, but my story was about the person who turned into a shark.

Oddly enough as I sat with *Turtle Diary* open in front of me seeing tenuous connections between my own childhood memories of sharks and my New Mexico fantasy, and Tolkein's speculations about desire, and the rich man lusting for the attention of the shark, I glanced at the opposite page where I absentmindedly read these lines.

> People write books for children and other people write books about the books written for children, but I don't think it's for the children at all. I think that all the people who worry so much about the children are really worrying about themselves, about keeping their world together and getting the children to help them do it, getting the children to agree that it is a world. Each new generation of children has to be told "This is a world, this is what one does, one lives like this." Maybe our constant fear is that a generation of children will come along and say "This is not a world, this is nothing, there is no way to live at all."

I can believe this, but I think Hoban has only told half the story. After all we don't simply tell children what is and is not true. They demand to be told. When a child writes and asks me "Do you believe in supernatural things?" they may be asking me to confirm that a story like *The Haunting* is literally true. But mostly they are asking "Just where am I to fit this story in my view of the world?" They want to be told what sort of world it is, and part of giving them the truest answer we can give also involves telling stories of desire: once there was a man who rode on a winged horse, once there was a boy who spoke to the animals, and the animals talked back to him, once there was a girl who grew so powerful that she was able not only to overcome her enemy but to overcome the base part of herself. Beware or the wolf will eat you and then you will become part of the wolf until something eats the wolf and so on. It is a gamble because we cannot tell just what is going to happen in the individual head when the story gets there and starts working. We can only predict statistically telling our children about hobbits or about atomic fission, or that the Earth fell off the Sun, or about photosynthesis, or that there was a loveable old archeologist called GUM who once adopted three little girls. Perhaps that is why I was so fascinated, long before I began to think on these subjects, by a line in Borges' story *Tlon Uqbar orbis tertius*. He writes about a land brought into existence by a sort of assertion "*The metaphysicians of Tlon are not looking for truth, nor even an approximation of it; they are after a kind of amazement.*"

I also believe that what I am looking for is truth, which by now I confidently expect to be more amazing than anything else.

These days it seems to me that when I look at the world I see many people, including politicians, television newsreaders, real estate agents, and free market financiers, librarians, too, at times, dressing as sharks, eating leaves and drinking out of puddles, casually taking over the powerful and dangerous forms that the imagination presents, eager to exploit the fictional forms that haunt us all, and sometimes becoming what in the beginning they only pretended to be. I once read that subatomic particles shouldn't be seen as tiny bits of matter but as mathematical singularities haunting space. I believe that inner space is haunted by other singularities, by stories, lines of power along which our lives align themselves like iron filings around a magnet defining the magnetic field by the patterns they form around it, and that we yearn for the structure stories confer, that we inhabit their patterns and often but not always, know instinctively how to use them well.

World Without, World Within

The mere cadence of six syllables—A Tale of Adventure—*instantly conjures up in the mind a jumbled and motley host of memories. Memories not only personal but we may well suspect racial; and not only racial but primeval. Ages before history had learned its letters, there being no letters to learn, ages before the children of men builded the city and the tower called Babel and their language was confounded, the rudiments of this kind of oral narrative must have begun to flourish. Indeed the greater part of even the largest of dictionaries, every page in the most comprehensive of atlases consists of relics and records in the concisest shorthand from bygone chapters of the tale whereof we know neither the beginning nor the end—that of Man's supreme venture into the world without and into the world within.*

Thank you very much.

Bibliography

Borges, Jorge Luis. "Tlon, Uqbar, Orbis, Tertius," in *Borges; A Reader*. E. P. Dutton, 1981.

De La Mare, Walter. *Desert Islands*. Faber and Faber, 1930.
Garner, Alan. "Achilles in Altjira," in *Innocence and Experience; Essays and Conversations on Children's Literature*. Lothrop, Lee and Shepard Books, 1987.
Hoban, Russell. *Turtle Diary*. Jonathan Cape, 1975.
Kepler, Johannes. *Astronomi Nova*.
Klotz, Irving M. "The N-ray Affair." *Scientific American*, May, 1980.
Streatfield, Noel. *Ballet Shoes*. Dent, 1936.
________. *The Whicharts*. Coward-McCann, 1931.
Tolkein, J.R.R. *Tree and Leaf*. Unwin Books, 1961.